Savior, REDEEMER of MY SOUL

Savior, REDEEMER of MY SOUL

KATHRYN JENKINS

CFI
An imprint of Cedar Fort, Inc.
Springville, Utah

Paperback ISBN 13: 978-1-4621-5050-2
eBooks ISBN 13: 978-1-4621-5051-9

Published by CFI, an imprint of Cedar Fort, Inc.
2373 W. 700 S., Suite 100, Springville, UT 84663
Distributed by Cedar Fort, Inc., www.cedarfort.com

Library of Congress Cataloging Number: 2025945537

Cover design by Shawnda T. Craig

Edited and Typeset by Liz Kazandzhy

Printed in the United States of America

10 9 8 7 6 5 4 3 2 1

Printed on acid-free paper

To Orson F. Whitney, whose dream and subsequent hymn inspired these words; and to my Savior and Redeemer, Jesus Christ, whose life and sacrifice give me an eternity of possibilities.

Contents

Introduction: Savior, Redeemer of My Soul

The lyrics to "Savior, Redeemer of My Soul"—one of the most stirring and sublime expressions of love for Jesus Christ—were penned by Orson F. Whitney, whose life was dedicated to serving the Lord. He served three full-time missions. His first was to Pennsylvania and Ohio. His second, two years after his marriage, was to London and Liverpool, England, during which he served as editor of the *Millennial Star.* His third was as president of the European Mission, a calling he fulfilled during his service as a member of the Quorum of the Twelve Apostles.

His was literally a lifetime of service as an influential and faithfully devoted Church leader. A few months after returning from his first mission and while still single, he was called to serve as bishop of the Eighteenth Ward in Salt Lake City, a calling he held for twenty-eight years. The authority who called him read a passage from the New Testament specifying that bishops are required to be married and then told him he ought to get married. (President Joseph Fielding Smith said of this, "It was the judgment of Paul that a deacon in that day should be a married man. That does not apply to our day."[1]) Less than a year later, Elder Whitney married Zina Beal Smoot.

After he was released as bishop, Elder Whitney served as assistant Church historian until his call to the Quorum of the Twelve in 1906. He served in that capacity until his death in 1931 at the age of seventy-five.

Elder Whitney's hymn expressed an unusually deep love of the Savior as well as heartfelt pleading to cultivate a life of devotion to the Redeemer. The power of his sentiments is wrapped up in the final stanza of his transcendent words: "Make me more worthy of Thy love | And fit me for the life above."[2]

Elder Whitney's deep love for the Savior may be due to a singular vision he had while serving his first mission.[3] Determined to become a newspaperman, Orson spent much of the first part of his mission in what he considered professional training—writing articles about Pennsylvania and Ohio for *The Salt Lake Tribune.* He didn't spend much time seeking converts.

All that changed one night when he received a remarkable vision. In that vision, it was the night of the Savior's sacrifice, and Orson found himself positioned in the Garden of Gethsemane at a spot where he could clearly see the Savior and hear His sacred appeal to the Father. As he described it, "As he [Christ] prayed the tears streamed down his face, which was toward me. I was so moved at the sight that I wept also, out of pure sympathy with his great sorrow. My whole heart went out to him. I loved him with all my soul and longed to be with him as I longed for nothing else."[4]

Suddenly the scene changed, and Orson found himself hidden behind a tree at the sacred place where the Savior gave His Apostles their charge to preach the gospel to all the world. As the Savior prepared to

1. *Answers to Gospel Questions,* comp. Joseph Fielding Smith (Deseret Book, 1957), 1:129.

2. "Savior, Redeemer of My Soul," *Hymns,* no. 112; text by Orson F. Whitney, music by Harry A. Dean.

3. See Dennis B. Horne, *The Life of Orson F. Whitney: Historian, Poet, Apostle, as Recorded in His Daily Journals* (Cedar Fort, 2014), as quoted in a review by Neal W. Kramer, *BYU Studies,* 57:3 (2018), 186–187.

4. Kramer, "Review of *The Life of Orson F. Whitney,*" 187–88.

ascend to heaven, Orson could not remain hidden any longer. In his words, "I ran out from behind the tree, fell at his feet, clasped him around the knees, and begged him to take me with him."

As Orson described it, the Savior stooped down, lifted him up, and embraced him. Orson said that the experience "was so vivid, so real, that I felt the very warmth of His bosom against which I rested."[5] The Savior's response inspired a new path of discipleship for Orson when He said, "No, my son; these [the Apostles] have finished their work, and they may go with me, but you must stay and finish yours."[6]

Overcome by love for the Savior and by an overpowering desire to be with Him, Orson clung to the Savior. Orson gazed up into His face and said, "Well, promise me that I will come to You at the last." The Savior made no such promise but sweetly and tenderly uttered six words that completely changed the trajectory of Orson Whitney's life: "That will depend entirely upon yourself."[7]

Orson said that he "awoke with a sob in [his] throat, and it was morning." Orson Whitney abandoned his newspaper work and, beginning that morning, started preaching the gospel and baptizing converts.

Perhaps it was that vision and the ensuing lifetime of dedicated service that instilled in Orson Whitney the deep and abiding love for the Savior that led him to write the moving words that became the hymn "Savior, Redeemer of My Soul." When he died in 1931, after serving twenty-five years as an Apostle, he was one of the most beloved leaders in the Church.

The first stanza of Orson Whitney's hymn says, simply, "Savior, Redeemer of My Soul." It was and has ever been the Father's design that the souls of humankind return to live with Him. His work and His glory, we are told, is "to bring to pass the immortality and eternal life of man" (Moses 1:39).

But that enterprise was never a simple one. Elder James E. Talmage testified that "without the aid of a power *above that of humanity* no soul would find its way back to God from whom it came. The need of

---

5. Orson F. Whitney, "The Divinity of Jesus Christ," *Ensign*, Dec. 2003, 10.
6. Kramer, "Review of *The Life of Orson F. Whitney*," 188.
7. Whitney, "The Divinity of Jesus Christ," 10.

a Redeemer lies in the inability of man to raise himself from the temporal to the spiritual plane, from the lower kingdom to the higher."[8]

The Father, who knows all things from the beginning (see 1 Nephi 9:6) and all things that are to come (see Words of Mormon 1:7), knew that we would be subject to sin, resulting in spiritual death. He also knew that His divine purpose required the Fall, which resulted in physical death. Finally, He knew that intertwined in it all would be Satan, whose purpose—directly opposed to that of the Father—was to make sure we *never* made it back home.

But in His incomprehensible love, the Father allowed for that. As Elder Talmage wrote, Satan's efforts "to make death inevitable, perpetual, and supreme were provided against *even before the first man had been created in the flesh*."[9] That allowance, our insurance against spiritual and physical death, was Jesus Christ.

As the prophet Nephi put it, "O how great the goodness of our God, who prepareth a way for our escape from the grasp of this awful monster; yea, that monster, death and hell" (2 Nephi 9:10).

Jesus Christ—the Savior, the Redeemer—was chosen and appointed to His mission by One greater than Himself: God the Father, whose works, designs, and purposes "cannot be frustrated, neither can they come to naught" (Doctrine and Covenants 3:1). With Him, our future is bright with hope; without Him, all of us would remain hopelessly in a fallen state.

Jesus was the Father's Only Begotten Son. Born of a mortal mother, Jesus "inherited the capacity to die; begotten by an immortal Sire He possessed as a heritage the power to withstand death indefinitely."[10] With His sacrifice in the Garden of Gethsemane, He paid the price for every sin, that no one would have to suffer if they would repent. On the cross at Golgotha, He *voluntarily* laid down His life so He could take it again. In the silence of the Garden Tomb, He

---

8. James E. Talmage, *Jesus the Christ* (The Church of Jesus Christ of Latter-day Saints, 1981), 27; emphasis added.
9. Talmage, 20; emphasis added.
10. Talmage, 22.

rose triumphant, the "firstfruits of them that slept" (1 Corinthians 15:20)—the first to pass from death to immortality.[11]

Mortal probation is so perilous—so rife with temptations and dangers—that all of us would be lost without a redeemer. As the Savior, Jesus Christ is also the Redeemer, one who redeems us from death, provides salvation from the effects of sin, and makes it possible for us to be exalted based on our righteous achievement during mortality.[12]

Jesus is the only one who is qualified to be the Redeemer. According to Elder Talmage, a redeemer must have been chosen in heaven and foreordained to redeem humankind; must be the Only Begotten of the Father, having attributes of both godhood and manhood; and must be the only sinless man who ever lived.[13] Without a redeemer—Jesus Christ, the Son of God—we could not have achieved exaltation under any circumstance.

As Alma testified, "There is no other way or means whereby man can be saved, only in and through Christ" (Alma 38:9). What He has done for us is immeasurable, staggering in its implications.

In every moment of His mortal life, He unflinchingly operated under the direction of the Father (see John 6:38). President John Taylor called Him "the author of eternal life and exaltation. He is the Redeemer, the Resurrector, the Savior of man and world . . . the Captain of our salvation . . . the Lord and Giver of life."[14]

As part of mortality, we are given law. We are free to obey or disobey that law. There is a consequence of everything we choose—either good (for obeying) or bad (for disobeying). It is part of the Father's plan that we are subjected to opposing influences—good and evil—so we can be tried and tested to determine whether we will "do all things whatsoever the Lord [our] God shall command [us]" (Abraham 3:25). Our agency, our freedom to choose, is a requisite part of the test of mortality.

The first such test of which we have record occurred in the Garden of Eden, when Lucifer beguiled Eve into partaking of the fruit of

---

11. See Talmage, 23.

12. See Talmage, 18.

13. See Talmage, 21.

14. John Taylor, *Mediation and Atonement* (Deseret News, 1878), 171.

the tree of knowledge of good and evil, which she and Adam had been commanded not to do. When Adam also partook of the fruit so the plan of salvation could be accomplished, death was introduced to the world (see Moses 4:17). Satan's role in the Fall must have been especially pleasing to him since he had been defeated by Michael—Adam—in the War in Heaven.

The Father, who knows all things (see 2 Nephi 9:20), knew what would happen in the Garden of Eden, and He was prepared. He provided a Savior, Jesus Christ, to redeem Adam and Eve and all of us from the effects of the Fall—both spiritual and physical death.

Of the redemptive nature of the Savior, Elder Talmage wrote, "The power of death was to be overcome, so that, though men would of necessity die, they would live anew, their spirits clothed with immortalized bodies over which death could not again prevail."[15] There is no mistake: Satan will be powerless—totally helpless and impotent—over those immortalized bodies. The outcome of the battle for our souls has already been decided—the Lord, our Savior and Redeemer, has the final victory.

Without the Savior, Adam and Eve and all of us would have remained in a fallen state, unable to return to our Father or gain exaltation. Because of the Savior, Adam and Eve and all of us are redeemed from the effects of the Fall *without our even seeking that redemption.* It is a gift freely given.

Without the Savior's Atonement, the creation of man would have been futile. The Atonement, which Elder Talmage calls voluntary and "love-inspired,"[16] provides salvation and relief from individual sin to all those who repent. It also provides universal redemption from the death invoked by the Fall. Because of Christ, all those who ever lived—not just the righteous—will be resurrected.

Every one of us stands in need of the Savior's Atonement because we are all sinners. And through the Savior, the Redeemer of our souls, we are given the chance for everlasting life and exaltation. For as the prophet Nephi wrote, "There is none other way nor name given under

---

15. Talmage, 18.
16. Talmage, 21.

heaven whereby man can be saved in the kingdom of God" (2 Nephi 31:21).

As William W. Phelps penned in the jubilant words of another hymn, "Redeemer of Israel, our only delight . . . Our King, our Deliverer, our all!"[17]

That Savior, that Redeemer, is Jesus Christ, the Son of the Living God. For us, He gave everything. To Him, we owe everything.

17. "Redeemer of Israel," *Hymns,* no. 6; text by William W. Phelps, music by Freeman Lewis.

Whose Mighty Hand Hath Made Me Whole

One of the most poignant stories from the life of the Savior is that of the man at the pool of Bethesda (see John 5:2–8). According to local legend, an angel periodically visited the pool and stirred up its waters. That same legend claimed that the first person to step into the water after it was stirred up would be healed of whatever disease he had. In other words, that person would be made whole.

Traveling to Jerusalem to attend one of the Jewish feasts, Jesus took a shortcut by walking through the five porches that surrounded the pool, which was located adjacent to the sheep market. We're told that in the shade of these porches "lay a great multitude of impotent folk, of blind, halt, withered, waiting for the moving of the water" (John 5:3). As He walked, Jesus passed that great multitude—but one in particular caught His attention.

We're never told the crippled man's name, but Jesus must have known it. Because Jesus knew that the crippled man had suffered from his infirmity for thirty-eight years (at a time when the average lifespan was thirty-five years!)—many of which had been spent at the edge of that pool, waiting with desperate hope for a miracle.

Jesus approached the man and asked if he wanted to be made whole. Made whole! It was the man's most fervent desire. But he answered Jesus simply: He had no one to help him down to the water when it was stirred up—no one to lower him into the pool. And by the time he crawled to the edge of the pool, another always got there first. The fervently hoped-for miracle had not happened.

After decades of trying, he had never been the first into the water. He had not been healed.

Jesus stood there looking at this pitiful man, whose wretched condition was truly heartbreaking. We can only imagine that the man's plight must have touched the Savior deeply.

The response of Jesus to this feeble man is instructive. Jesus could have summoned someone to help the man down to the water. Or the Savior Himself could have waited with the man and carried him to the pool as soon as the waters were stirred. But He chose a better way.

Knowing the man wanted to be made whole, Jesus simply said to him, "Rise, take up thy bed, and walk" (John 5:8).

And so the man stood, picked up his bed, and walked. He received his miracle—not in the swirling waters of the pool but at the hand of the Healer of all humankind. This account reminds me that as I wait to be made whole, it may happen in a way I am totally not expecting.

The man at the pool of Bethesda had no power to come to Jesus. Instead, Jesus came to him and made him whole.

He will do the same for all of us.

Sometimes I forget how much I mean to the Savior. In my own distressing times, I don't remember the greatest distress ever experienced—don't remember that Jesus anguished in the garden, bleeding great drops of blood from every pore due to the intensity of His pain, just to give *me* the opportunity to repent. That He hung for six hours after being flogged and brutally nailed to a cross for *me.* I meant that much to Him. I still do. And so do you.

I am reminded that, as C. S. Lewis wrote, Jesus "died not for men, but for each man. If each man had been the only man made, He would have done no less."[18] On another occasion, Lewis wrote a

18. C. S. Lewis, *Perelandra* (Scribner, 1943).

similar sentiment: "When Christ died, He died for you individually just as much as if you'd been the only [person] in the world."[19]

It's as though I'm the only person here—the only person He was determined to save. It's the same for you.

I am reminded too that through some divine arithmetic, not even a sparrow can fall to the ground without His notice—and that the very hairs on my head are numbered to Him (see Matthew 10:29 30).

I am of infinite importance to Him. So are you. A popular Christian hymn tells us, "His eye is on the sparrow, and I know He watches me."[20]

If you have a difficult time believing that, remember what happened to Bartimaeus. On the Savior's final journey to Jerusalem, He passed through Jericho. As He came out of the city, He was accompanied by a large group of people, as was often the case at that time in His ministry.

As He walked, He passed a man who seemed as though he had been thrown by the side of the road like a pitiful piece of litter. It was Bartimaeus, a blind man who sat amid the debris on the roadside and who made his living by begging—the only thing he was capable of doing. Hearing the commotion, Bartimaeus asked those around him what was happening. When he learned that Jesus of Nazareth was walking by, hope flooded his soul.

Suddenly, he became animated and cried with a loud voice, "Jesus, thou Son of David, have mercy on me" (Mark 10:47). I can't even imagine the excitement Bartimaeus must have felt at that moment. Since Bartimaeus called the Savior the "Son of David," it's clear that Bartimaeus knew of Jesus and believed Him to be the Messiah. It's also obvious that Bartimaeus believed in Jesus's willingness and ability to help at a time when most religious leaders attributed blindness (and similar afflictions) to God's judgment for sin or other misdeeds.

Those who were walking with Jesus told Bartimaeus to quiet down and stop calling out to the Savior. They saw him as nothing more than an irritation, an annoying thing that would do nothing more than

19. C. S. Lewis, *Mere Christianity* (HarperCollins, 1952).

20. "His Eye Is on the Sparrow," lyrics by Civilla D. Martin, 1905; music by Charles H. Gabriel, 1905.

interrupt the Savior's intended journey. That's how it is with men and women of the world—too often, it's far too easy for them to dismiss the pain and struggle of others.

But Bartimaeus would not be deterred. He only cried out louder, repeating his original request. We assume that his voice reflected what was in his heart—that he was longing for help from the Lord. Though others started ridiculing him for making so much noise, he was undeterred. As President Spencer W. Kimball noted, Bartimaeus demonstrated "persistent, faithful efforts to reach the Lord" with his petitions.[21] Such might be a pattern for us.

The people with Jesus may have been able to write off Bartimaeus, but the Savior was not. To Him, the beggar was not an irritation but was like a crying child. Jesus stopped. He stood still. He then commanded those with Him to bring the blind man to Him.

Suddenly, Bartimaeus was elevated in the minds of the others. Jesus had noticed him—had invited him to approach! Where they had previously tried to quiet him, now the people around Bartimaeus told him, "Be of good comfort, rise; he calleth thee" (Mark 10:49).

Then the Gospel writer Mark specifies an interesting thing: Bartimaeus rose and went to Jesus, but only after "casting away his garment" (Mark 10:50). Like those of other beggars, the garment of Bartimaeus was likely tattered and soiled and maybe even decayed in places—trodden under foot, much like Bartimaeus himself. By casting it off, Bartimaeus was symbolically casting off his old life as he approached the man of God, brimming with faith and anticipation.

Facing the blind man with the utmost compassion, Jesus asked what Bartimaeus wanted Him to do. Bartimaeus's request was simple and clear: "Lord, that I might receive my sight" (Mark 10:51). The blind man—a beggar by profession—could have asked for food or money, but his faith was far greater than that; he asked for his sight. He also could have tempered his request with words that would have justified his request. Instead, he simply expressed his sincere desire, believing that Jesus was not only willing but able to grant it. Bartimaeus

21. "President Kimball Speaks Out on Administration to the Sick," *New Era*, Oct. 1981, 47.

demonstrated unequivocal faith in the Healer. The same kind of faith we should have. Faith in His ability to make us whole.

Touching the blind man's eyes, Jesus said, "Go thy way; thy faith hath made thee whole" (Mark 10:52). And what of Bartimaeus? He *immediately* received his sight. And, incidentally, instead of darting off in joy over all the things he could now do, he chose instead to follow Jesus (see Mark 10:52).

If Bartimaeus had been afraid to call out, had he been quieted by his friends, or had he questioned the Savior's willingness to act, he would have stayed blind forever. His own fear and doubts would have prevented the miracle. Instead, he understood the truth that God rewards those who earnestly seek him (see Hebrews 11:6). Just as what happened to Bartimaeus, when we earnestly seek Him, He can—and will—make us whole.

If Jesus was able to hear that solitary voice through the tumult of the crowds and cared enough to heal a poor, filthy beggar, certainly He can hear me. He can hear you. We may not comprehend such with our mortal understanding, but He can hear our cries for help through the mayhem and commotion of an entire universe filled with those who might also be calling out for relief. To Him, it is as though every one of us is the only one. The very hairs of our head are numbered to Him.

And remembering the story of Bartimaeus, I have to ask myself: What do *I* do when I am made whole? Do I cast aside my worldly pursuits, like Bartimaeus cast aside his garment, and instead follow the One who made me whole?

Another of Jesus's miracles should remind all of us of the importance of the one.

It would be difficult for most of us to imagine what the past twelve years had been like for a woman who goes unnamed but who is identified as the woman with an issue of blood. Now, twelve years into her malady, she likely suffered extreme weakness, fatigue, anemia, a rapid heartbeat, low blood pressure, and low body temperature, among other problems associated with her blood loss.

Doctors of that day were relatively unskilled; surgery was a last resort because there was no anesthesia, and most of those who underwent surgery died of shock as a result. Simply put, the "cure" was often worse than the illness itself.

Many who practiced medicine at that time had no training; some Jewish rabbis posed as physicians even though they had no applicable schooling. One of the treatments for women with chronic bleeding shows how primitive the remedies of that day were. The woman was to dig seven pits, and in each pit, she was to burn vine branches that were not yet four years old. Carrying a cup of wine, she was to approach each pit in succession, sit down by the side of it, and chant, "Be free from thy sickness."

According to Jewish law, the woman with the issue of blood was ceremonially unclean because of her bleeding (see Leviticus 15:25). Consider what that meant: For twelve long years, she had been unable to live a normal life. She couldn't associate with others or enter a synagogue to worship God. She could not go to the market or draw water from the well. Even in her own home, she could not care for her children, cook or serve food to members of her family, or engage in intimate relations. Anything she lay or sat on became unclean, as did anyone she touched. (In case you're thinking that women were treated unfairly, men who had an issue of blood were subject to even stricter guidelines.)

This woman had spent all her money in search of a cure, but nothing had helped her. Because her condition had persisted for twelve long years, it's easy to presume that she was desperate—physically, mentally, emotionally, and even spiritually spent. I can also realistically believe that she felt helpless and hopeless—*until* she heard about Jesus. She knew that He was going to be walking through her village, and she was determined to find Him.

According to the laws of ritual purity, she should not have even ventured out into the crowd that day, let alone touched anyone, so it must have taken great courage, determination, and desperation for her to press through the throngs toward Jesus. But she had faith in Him. She knew that if she could just touch the hem of His clothing, she would be healed. He was her last hope. Her faith was so great that she didn't even need to speak to Him—she believed she would be healed if she could merely touch a piece of His robe. Just the hem of His garment.

In some amazing feat of resolve, she did reach the Savior. She touched His robe. He was so aware of her touch that He immediately knew someone had touched Him (see Luke 8:46). When Jesus asked who it was that had touched Him, He wasn't seeking information. He already knew. He asked so she could publicly testify of the miracle that had taken place. He wanted everyone there—and all of us—to know that the miracle was *not* the result of magic or sorcery, which were common in the ancient world, but of faith.

Of her faith. And His.

As with the woman who pressed through the crowds toward Jesus, we can know that He "shall wipe away all tears from [our] eyes; and there shall be no more death, neither sorrow, nor crying, neither . . . pain" (Revelation 21:4). We will, in every sense of the word, be made whole.

When we demonstrate our willingness to follow, His mighty hand will, according to His will, heal our bodies and our spirits. Will cast off our infirmities. Will make us gloriously whole.

His mighty hand has made me whole—physically, emotionally, and spiritually—more times than these pages have room to contain. But one in particular stands out in my mind.

I was addressing a group of seventeen-year-old youth in Salt Lake City as a guest speaker one morning on how to spiritually prepare to serve a mission. The central message I wanted to convey was that once they received a mission call, the adversary would do everything possible to derail them—to keep them from taking their message to the world. I warned that could even include tempting them to do things that might make them unworthy.

I had testified of repentance and said that each of us can be made whole, whatever the problems of the past.[22] Suddenly, my voice sounded to me as though it was at the end of a very long tunnel. I glanced down at my notes, and they were so garbled that I couldn't make sense of them. They didn't even resemble the alphabet with which I was familiar. Then profuse, ice-cold sweat began pouring down my face. Then I couldn't speak. At all.

---

22. See Jeffrey R. Holland, *Created for Greater Things* (Deseret Book, 2011).

In reality, that probably lasted less than a minute—but to me, standing in front of that group, it felt like forever. I've concluded that the youth in that audience simply thought I was choked up from feeling the Spirit. When I was finally able to speak again, I thought, *Kathy, this can't be good. Wrap it up and sit down.*

I tried to summarize the remaining fourth of my carefully prepared presentation into a few sentences, concluded with a rapid testimony, and sat down in a chair just behind the podium.

The youth, seemingly unfazed, gathered around a table in the back for orange juice and cookies. The stake president, whom I had never met, rushed through the throng to me and asked with some urgency, "Did you just have a stroke?"

"I—I don't know," I answered truthfully. I didn't know *what* had happened. Nothing like that had ever happened to me before.

"Would you like me to call an ambulance?"

Oh, wow, I thought. *He's serious. He's really worried.*

I assured him that I thought I'd be okay—that I just needed to sit quietly for a minute.

Sure enough, whatever it was passed fairly quickly, and I felt much better. Almost normal. I was supposed to stay at the conference to hear the next few presentations and then enjoy lunch with the youth, but I thought I'd better call it a day. I sought out the stake president and graciously excused myself, saying I thought I'd better go home.

"Home" was in Orem, Utah, forty miles to the south.

"You can't drive home!" he exclaimed.

"I think I'll be fine," I said, for the moment really believing that. He shook his head and tried several more times to dissuade me as he walked me to the outside door of the hotel where the conference was being held. Thanking him, I headed to my car.

As soon as I sat down in the driver's seat, I thought, *You can't drive home.* I called a good friend, Kimball, who lived in Salt Lake's Avenues. Without telling him any details, I told him where I was and asked if he could give me a priesthood blessing so I could drive home. He readily agreed.

A few minutes later, he pulled up next to my car. Scrambling out of his car, he told me, "I said a prayer before leaving home so I could give you a blessing. I was told you need to go to the hospital on 5300 South. You need to go *now*. I'll give you a blessing when we get there."

I objected. He insisted. Finally accepting that he was intent on getting me to a hospital, I suggested LDS Hospital instead; I'd been a patient there several years earlier for a knee replacement, and they already had information about me. Kimball simply looked at me, astonishment on his face, and said, "Kathy, *I was told the hospital on 5300 South*. Let me drive your car."

When we arrived at the emergency room and checked in, Kimball asked if there was a quiet room where he could give me a blessing. There was. The blessing offered the promise of health. I was then whisked to an examination room.

For seven hours, one test after another was conducted. A flurry of nurses, physician assistants, and doctors attended to me. Kimball patiently kept vigil in the waiting room, despite my frequent requests that he take my car and leave. I promised to call him when I was ready to be picked up. He refused to go.

Finally, a stern-faced doctor told me, "We don't know for sure what's wrong, but it's serious. We're going to admit you so we can run more tests." Kimball bid me farewell, and I was taken to a room.

Subsequent tests over the next few days revealed the extent of the problem. I had suffered a heart attack *and* a stroke. Attempting to drive home, the doctor told me, would have rapidly gone from foolish to fatal.

The Lord had started exercising His mighty hand on my behalf. That hospital—the one Kimball had been instructed to take me to—was the leading heart treatment hospital for a five-state area. Had I gone anywhere else, even LDS Hospital just fifty-three blocks away, I would have been life-flighted to the hospital in which I found myself. The doctor who was "randomly" assigned to me in the emergency room was a top-flight, well-respected cardiothoracic surgeon sought by patients throughout that five-state area and even some from outside the country.

He explained that all five of my coronary arteries were 90 percent blocked and that I needed coronary bypass surgery. Then he asked a question that stunned me: "When did you have your previous heart attack?"

I told him I'd never had a heart attack. And I was sure I hadn't. *He* was sure I *had*—tests showed with clarity a fairly large spot on my heart that was dead. Not from what had just happened but from a much older episode.

"That's going to complicate the bypass," he said, "but I think we can work around it."

Because of wildly fluctuating blood sugar and blood pressure, I was in the hospital for eleven days before they could stabilize me enough to do the surgery. The night before I was to be taken to the operating room, Kimball gave me another blessing. The Lord promised a successful surgery and recovery.

The first thing I remember when coming out of anesthesia after the twelve-hour surgery was my surgeon, leaning down close to my face and saying, "That was amazing. I got in there, and the dead tissue in your heart was gone. Just gone. Your heart was pristine. I've never seen anything like it."

The Lord, with His mighty hand, had made me whole.

I stayed in the hospital for nine days after the surgery. There were some complications, and my normal heart rhythm had to be restored. After I got home, an infection in one of the incisions in my leg where they harvested my vein got infected with *E. coli*, a situation so serious that I was told I could lose my leg—or my life. I lost neither and underwent an additional surgery, thanks to the mighty hand of the Lord.

He made me whole.

In the four years since, I've had other unrelated health complications, several of which should have killed me. But they didn't. And through it all, my heart has continued beating in my chest, strong and sure.

Why?

The Lord. The hairs of my head are numbered to Him, and it's as if I were the only one here. He cares that much and is that deeply involved.

His mighty hand has made me whole. Just as it will do for you. For all of us.

Whose Wondrous Power Hath Raised Me Up

To *raise* means to move to a higher position—to elevate, lift up, set upright.

Whenever I think of the power required to lift, my mind races back almost five decades to a once-in-a-lifetime trip I took to Greece. The highlight of that journey was standing in front of what until then I had seen only in books—the magnificent Parthenon, built as a temple to the goddess Athena and considered the greatest example of Greek architecture in existence. Sitting atop the Acropolis, the highest point in Athens, the stunning structure could be seen from any location in the city.

Just below the Parthenon is a barren outcropping of rock known as Mars Hill. It's where the Apostle Paul preached the sermon found in Acts 17, teaching the doctrine that we are the literal offspring of God. The experience of being there was both overwhelming and magnificent.

Construction of the Parthenon began in 447 BC using marble from the quarries of Mount Penteli. The marble was moved from the quarries to the temple site by more than 600 skilled laborers and 150 marble workers. The completed Parthenon consisted of more than

16,500 pieces of marble and, surprisingly, took only nine years to build.

What captured my imagination most was the roof—or, more accurately, the absence of the roof. Just three centuries after Christ walked the dusty trails of the Holy Land, a fire destroyed much of the interior of the building and completely demolished the roof. Builders replaced the original marble roof with a new wooden one covered with clay tiles.

But how, marveled our tour guide, were those builders raised to the height of the roof so they could accomplish that repair? Even more puzzling, how did the original builders get to the top of the structure, forty-five feet off the ground, to construct a heavy marble roof?

During the ensuing centuries, the Parthenon was used as an Islamic mosque, a Christian church, and a Catholic church. But all that changed in the late 1600s.

It seems that during a war that began in 1684, the Ottoman Turks decided to use the Parthenon not only as shelter for the local Turkish community but as a place to store their gunpowder. They felt sure their enemy, the Venetians, would never attack a structure of such historic significance. A temple.

They were wrong.

The Venetians found out about the gunpowder. And on September 26, 1687, they fired a mortar round from a nearby hill, blowing up the entire stockpile of gunpowder. Three of the four walls in the center of the Parthenon crumbled into rubble, and three-fifths of the sculptures inside the structure toppled to pieces. And the roof? Not a single part of the roof remained intact.

For three and a half centuries, the Parthenon stood as it appeared following the mortar attack in 1687. One of the issues, our tour guide told us, was that *even with modern technology and equipment*, no one could figure out how to raise a new roof.

Restoration efforts finally began in the late nineteenth century, when some of the interior walls were restored—but incorrectly. In 1992 and 1993, those walls were dismantled and properly restored. In 2019, almost fifty years after I visited it, comprehensive restoration began in earnest, including the placement of overlapping marble tiles on a roof.

Raising the roof became possible this time through the use of recently developed industrial cranes.

It takes great power—almost incomprehensible power—to raise many things. I remember the feat of engineering required to raise the corner of my friend's house when she found out that the foundation beneath it was sagging. I remember watching as the new angel Moroni statue—weighing somewhere between one and two tons—was raised to the top of the Oquirrh Mountain Temple to replace the original, which was scorched and blackened by a lightning strike.

I remember many times when I have been raised—spiritually, emotionally—by the wondrous power of the Lord. His was the only power that could have raised me during those wrenching times.

I am certainly not alone. There are numerous examples throughout the scriptures of those who were raised by the Lord's wondrous power. One of my favorites is that of a young David—a slight shepherd boy inexperienced in battle—who found himself facing the towering, menacing giant, Goliath.

In that day, armies were often quite small. It wasn't unusual for each army to select one warrior to represent it in a one-on-one battle against the other army's representative. The two chosen representatives faced off as their respective armies watched from the sidelines. Tradition had it that the outcome of that contest determined which army won the battle.

The Philistines had come to war against the house of Israel, and up thundered the representative of the Philistines—a giant named Goliath, who stood, from what we can tell, nine feet and nine inches tall. He was fully outfitted in armor that weighed an estimated hundred and fifty pounds; his iron spearhead alone weighed between twelve and twenty-six pounds. He was powerful, brutal, well-exercised in battle, and ferociously loyal to the Philistines, who had a long history of conflict with the house of Israel.

After setting out his intention to win victory for the Philistines, Goliath walked down to a valley and bellowed toward the opposing army, "I defy the armies of Israel this day; give me a man, that we may fight together" (1 Samuel 17:10). Upon seeing the armor-clad giant, the armies of the house of Israel were "dismayed, and greatly afraid" (1 Samuel 17:11). Who could blame them?

It's no wonder that the Philistines chose Goliath to represent them in this pivotal contest.

And it's no wonder that none of the Israelites wanted to fight him.

No Israelite stepped forward that first day. In fact, Goliath issued his challenge every day for forty days. The Philistines were camped on a mountain on one side of a valley, and the Israelites were camped on a mountain on the other side. For forty days, Goliath came down to the valley every morning and every evening and challenged the house of Israel to send out a representative so they could fight.

David was among those numbered in the army of the house of Israel. He was conscripted with his three older brothers. But because he was the youngest and was a shepherd by trade, he regularly left the army's station and returned home to tend the sheep.

One day when he returned from tending the sheep, he brought corn, cheese, and loaves of bread back to the army. He arrived just as Goliath again came down to the valley and shouted his usual challenge. David watched as all the men in the army of Israel did what they had been doing for the previous forty days when they saw Goliath—they "fled from him, and were sore afraid" (1 Samuel 17:24).

Seeing that no one else was willing to face off against Goliath, David went to the Israelite captain, Saul, and volunteered to take up the cause. Saul was incredulous. "Thou art not able to go against this Philistine to fight with him," Saul told David, "for thou art but a youth, and he a man of war from his youth" (1 Samuel 17:33).

David then gave a convincing argument for himself. He told Saul that once while he was tending his father's sheep, a lion and a bear came into the flock and took a lamb. David ran after the lion, smote him, and took the lamb out of his mouth. When the lion fought back, the young shepherd grabbed him by his mane and killed him. He also killed the bear.

David finished his account by telling Saul, "The Lord that delivered me out of the paw of the lion, and out of the paw of the bear, he will deliver me out of the hand of this Philistine" (1 Samuel 17:37).

At that, Saul acquiesced and told David, "Go, and the Lord be with thee" (1 Samuel 17:37). Saul armed David with his own protective covering, fitting him with a coat of mail and putting a brass helmet on his head. But David took off all of Saul's armor and approached the giant Philistine with no more than five smooth stones and a sling.

David was no stranger to slinging stones. Most shepherds used slings to drive straying sheep back to the pasture and to protect the flock from wolves and other predatory animals. Most slings of that day were made of leather and consisted of a pouch with strings attached to each side. The pouch was whirled overhead until it reached a certain speed, at which time one string was released, launching the stone toward its target.

David had confidence in his ability with a sling. He'd had plenty of practice. But his real confidence was in the power of the Lord. As he approached the giant in the valley, Goliath laughed with derision, telling David, "Come to me, and I will give thy flesh unto the fowls of the air, and to the beasts of the field" (1 Samuel 17:44).

With complete faith in the Lord's power to raise him up to the challenge, David responded, "Thou comest to me with a sword, and with a spear, and with a shield: but I come to thee in the name of the Lord of hosts, the God of the armies of Israel, whom thou hast defied. *This day will the Lord deliver thee into mine hand* . . . that all the earth may know that there is a God in Israel" (1 Samuel 17:45–46; emphasis added).

With that, Goliath started toward David. And David? While the rest of his army had consistently cowered at the thought of confronting the giant, David *ran* to meet his daunting opponent on the field. He quickly placed a round, smooth stone in the sling and propelled it toward the giant. The stone sunk into Goliath's forehead, and he fell face-first to the ground. David stood on the giant's back and cut off the man's head with Goliath's own sword.

When the Philistine army saw what had happened, they fled. The victory went to the Israelites—but, in all reality, the victory was the Lord's. It belonged to Him whose wondrous power raised up a humble, simple shepherd to accomplish a mighty work.

Most of my life, I'd heard the saying, "The Lord will never give you more than you can bear." At first, I accepted that at face value. It sounded nice; I could easily believe that a loving, merciful Savior would feel that way. And that's not all; it gave me hope. In those moments when I really struggled, I held tight to that sentiment, believing that whatever was happening was *not* beyond my ability to withstand.

One day, driven to the scriptures in the midst of a particularly difficult circumstance, I decided to find that bit of holy writ that I'd carried around in my head and heart for so many years. I wanted to get the exact wording—the chapter and verse. And guess what? After an exhaustive search, I couldn't find it. It wasn't in the scriptures.

This can't be. I've known this—heard *this—all my life.*

But then I started thinking. I thought about Job, the Old Testament prophet known for his complete integrity, the father of seven sons and three daughters, the wealthy owner of lands and herds. He was a righteous man who "feared God, and eschewed evil" (Job 1:1). When Satan received permission from the Lord to tempt and try Job (see Job 1:12; 2:6), Job lost all that he had—seven thousand sheep, three thousand camels, five hundred yokes of oxen, and five hundred female donkeys—as well as all his servants. It didn't stop there; he also lost his children. Then he was covered with boils from the soles of his feet to the top of his head.

I think Job would have taken exception to the saying that we would never be given more than we could bear.

And what about the Apostle Paul who, describing his missionary labors in Asia, reported that "we were pressed out of measure, above strength, insomuch that we despaired even of life"? (2 Corinthians 1:8). I think Paul too would have questioned such a simplistic belief.

Then I thought of a man who was driven from one home after another. Who buried his babies in tiny graves. Who was tarred and feathered. Who spent an inhumane winter in a damp dungeon called Liberty, where he was fed rotten food and was unable to stand upright. Who, mortally wounded, fell from an upper-story window in the jail at Carthage.

I think Joseph Smith would also have taken exception to that same cliché.

I started looking at the people around me. At myself. At Job and Paul and Joseph. At life. And I started to seriously question that well-worn adage. I saw in myself and in those around me that we *were* often given things that pushed us up against the very edge of what we could bear—and sometimes, very realistically, into acres of pain that we couldn't bear.

Things like infidelity.

Financial ruin.

Estrangement from those closest to us.

A cancer diagnosis.

The death of a loved one.

A prodigal child.

And any of a countless number of other circumstances that could lay siege to any one of us at a moment's notice.

No. I and others I knew so well seemed to have been given more than anyone could bear.

But we *can* withstand whatever is given us with *the other part of the equation.*

Job, Paul, the Prophet Joseph, and countless others have recognized that *other* part of the equation: The Lord will never give us more than we can bear *with Him.*

On our own, just like the shepherd boy David, there is much we might not be able to bear. But when the Lord raises us up, as He did David, there is nothing we can't bear.

Look at Hezekiah, who became king of Judah at the tender age of twenty-five. That would have been no easy task considering his age alone but the difficulty of what he faced was infinitely compounded by what was going on in Judah when he became king. His predecessor, Ahaz, had driven the nation into wickedness. He had desecrated the temple, made and worshipped idols, sacrificed children, and burned incense not in the temple but "in the high places, and on the hills, and under every green tree" (2 Chronicles 28:4).

The Lord's anger was kindled by all that was happening, and He allowed the kings of Syria and Israel to smite Judah with a "great slaughter" (2 Chronicles 28:5); 120,000 "valiant men" were killed in a single day. An additional 200,000 women and children were taken away captive.

Ahaz reacted by doing everything he could think of to placate the king of the Assyrians, including making sacrifices to their gods. He also destroyed the vessels in the temple, put out the lamps, stopped burning incense there, and shut its doors. In its place, he made high places where he could burn incense and made altars in every corner of Jerusalem.

When Ahaz died, they buried him in Jerusalem—but not in the sepulchres where the other kings had been laid to rest. That's when Hezekiah became king, and the land he inherited was one marked by chaos, wickedness, and unrest.

But Hezekiah, we are told, "did that which was right in the sight of the Lord" (2 Chronicles 29:2). In his very first month on the throne, he opened the doors of the temple and repaired the damage that had been done. He then gathered the priests and the Levites and challenged them to first sanctify themselves, then to sanctify the temple and "carry forth the filthiness out of the holy place" (2 Chronicles 29:5). It was his intention, he told them, to "make a covenant with the Lord God of Israel, that his fierce wrath may turn away from us" (2 Chronicles 29:10).

After cleansing the temple, Hezekiah restored the dignity of the priesthood, reinstituted the Feast of the Passover, and brought the people together in worship.

But in the midst of Hezekiah's efforts to restore righteousness to Judah, his kingdom was attacked by the Assyrians, who swept into Judah and captured forty-one cities, including Jerusalem. When he realized that the armies were advancing and were determined to conquer as many cities as possible, Hezekiah worked with his people to do what they could to prepare for the attacks. First, they dammed the brook and the fountains so the invading army would have no water. They repaired the walls surrounding the cities, fortified them with towers, and made "darts and shields in abundance" (2 Chronicles 32:5). Then he appointed captains of war over the people.

Despite their rigorous preparations, the people were gripped with fear by the size and the ferocity of the invading army that waited just outside the walls, poised to attack. They were outnumbered, and they knew it. The opposing army was more experienced. Had more weapons. Hezekiah's army could have well feared that this was more than they could bear.

But then Hezekiah told them to be "strong and courageous, be not afraid nor dismayed for the king of Assyria, nor for all the multitude that is with him: for there be more with us than with him. With him is an arm of flesh; but with us is the Lord our God to help us, and to fight our battles" (2 Chronicles 32:7–8).

On another occasion, the king of Assyria sent an army to capture not only Israel but the prophet Elisha in particular. The colossal Assyrian army approached by night, consisting of vast numbers of horses, chariots, and warriors (see 2 Kings 6:14).

When Elisha rose early the next morning, he saw that the city was completely surrounded. As Elisha gazed at the armies, his terrified servant approached him and asked what they could do about the impending battle.

Elisha, who knew the other part of the equation, answered, "Fear not: for they that be with us are more than they that be with them" (2 Kings 6:16). Elisha then prayed that the Lord might open the eyes of the servant so he could see what Elisha himself could see. And the servant "saw: and, behold, the mountain was full of horses and chariots of fire round about Elisha" (2 Kings 6:17).

Not just chariots. *Chariots of fire.*

In your own struggle, remember Hezekiah and Elisha and chariots of fire as far as the eye can see.

One of my favorite hymns was inspired by the prophet Isaiah, who said of the Lord, the God of the Old Testament, "Fear thou not; for I am with thee: be not dismayed; for I am thy God: I will strengthen thee; yea, I will help thee; yea, I will uphold thee with the right hand of my righteousness" (Isaiah 41:10). How often I have been brought out of a swamp of fear and dismay to be strengthened beyond any capability of my own by He who has raised me and upheld me with the wondrous power of His mighty hand.

One such time comes particularly to mind. Reflecting on it, I might have personified Lemony Snicket's series of unfortunate events—or, as came from the pen of Judith Viorst, my own terrible, horrible, no good, very bad day. Only mine lasted not a day but eighteen months. And at the time, it seemed truly awful. I'll touch on only a few of the things that happened.

My "series of unfortunate events" began on my birthday in 2002 (it still takes me by surprise when I realize it was more than two decades ago!) when my seventeen-year-old son took his own life. An elderly birdwatcher, peering through binoculars at a grove of trees in a vacant lot, saw my son dangling at the end of a rope. Responding paramedics were able to get him down and away from the site just minutes before the bell sounded, dismissing elementary school children from a mere block away who walked home along the edge of that lot. A tender mercy.

Sometime later, my husband left the Church and our family, revealing heartbreaking betrayal. A few months after that, I was laid off from an excellent-paying job I'd had for fourteen years. With the company facing substantial budget cuts, I was one of hundreds let go. With no alimony and no child support from my divorce, it was a difficult time to face unemployment. But thankfully, I was given a generous severance package that sustained me for four months. Another tender mercy.

Just as my funds were running out, and two days after I was hired by an energetic entrepreneurial company, my twenty-year-old son died in the early hours of the morning on our family room couch of an accidental drug overdose.

Put together, that series of events might have been more than I could bear—on my own. In fact, I'm sure it would have been more than I could bear on my own. But I *wasn't* alone. The Lord was with me, and as I gazed out on *those* acres of pain, I could see horses and chariots of fire, more than I could count. They that were with me were *more*. Were enough. Raised me up.

It was absolutely wondrous.

One of my favorite scriptures cites the Lord's promise to missionaries, though each of us can call on the same assurance: "And whoso receiveth you, there I will be also, for I will go before your face. I will be on your right hand and on your left, and my Spirit shall be in your hearts, and *mine angels round about you, to bear you up*" (Doctrine and Covenants 84:88; emphasis added).

There are countless examples of missionaries who were raised up by the Lord and His angels. My son's missionary journals are filled with accounts of such things. My husband related the way in which the Lord raised him up while he was preparing for his own mission by placing within his circle of influence people who led him to profound truths. Many of these came from completely unexpected places. One was the owner of a small bookstore near my husband's home who took the time to introduce him to classic doctrinal works; he was also willing to spend hours discussing truths with my husband as the eyes of my husband's understanding were opened. Another was a teaching assistant in a math class my husband took at the University of Utah; he patiently taught of the ten tribes as the two of them talked one day after class, a kernel that led my husband to further energizing research.

As he subsequently served a two-year mission in Germany, he found that everything he had picked up and studied was inspired to enable him to effectively teach the Catholics of southern Germany. As the Lord raised him up, the things he had studied were brought to his remembrance in a way that testified of the Lord's wondrous power.

The lives of early Church members are also replete with such examples. When Heber C. Kimball was called to serve a mission in England in 1837, it might have been more than he could have borne on his own. President Gordon B. Hinckley explained that Heber's mission "meant leaving a family destitute. It meant traveling to New York and crossing the sea when he had no money. It meant that a man with very little schooling, who had grown up and lived in frontier communities, would go to the great cities of the British Isles among a people known for their education and enlightenment."[23]

Heber himself wrote that the very idea of such a mission "was almost more than I could bear up under. I was almost ready to sink under the burden which was placed upon me." But Heber C. Kimball had access to the same thing we all do: the wondrous power of the Lord. He wasn't facing those extremities on his own. He accepted the call, sailed to England, and leaped from the ship when it docked in Liverpool.

What made the difference? Heber C. Kimball believed that the Lord "would support me by His almighty power, and endow me with every qualification that I needed."[24] He knew he would be strengthened, raised up.

---

23. Gordon B. Hinckley, "The Lengthened Shadow of the Hand of God," *Ensign*, May 1987, 53.

24. *History of the Church*, 2:489–490.

And he was. Within eight months, two thousand people were baptized, and twenty-six congregations of the Church were organized.[25] What the Lord did for Heber C. Kimball, He will do for all of us who trust in Him.

You are qualified in every way to have the Lord's wondrous power raise you up. Maybe what you are facing almost defies description—the death of a loved one, the loss of your home, the diagnosis of a terminal illness. Or maybe what you are facing isn't magnified on the world's stage but represents a harrowing Gethsemane to you—the dark passages of depression, the heartache of a prodigal child, the fear of failing an important exam.

Here is the good news in every challenge we face: The Lord wants you to rely on *His* strength, not your own. He wants you to hand it over to Him. He invites you and me and all of us to cast our cares upon Him (see 1 Peter 5:7). Doing so brings all of us to a point where "we [might] not trust in ourselves, but in God" (2 Corinthians 1:9).

You and I and all of us will partake of His wondrous power as we are raised to contend with all that faces us. For we are not alone, and when the Lord raises us up, there is nothing we cannot do.

---

25. See *Church History in the Fulness of Times* (The Church of Jesus Christ of Latter-day Saints, 2000), 176.

And Filled with Sweet My Bitter Cup

Adoniram Judson was one of the first Christian missionaries from America to be sent overseas. He entered what is now Brown University at the age of sixteen and graduated as valedictorian of his class at the age of nineteen. During his final year at Andover Theological Seminary, he dedicated himself to God and decided on a missionary career.

In 1812, just a few months after marrying his wife, Ann Hasseltine, he was sent to Burma, where he served as a Christian missionary for almost forty years.

Ann and three of their children died while Adoniram was serving in Burma. When a fellow missionary, Sarah Boardman, lost her husband, Adoniram penned a letter to her in which he wrote:

> You are now drinking the bitter cup whose dregs I am somewhat acquainted with. And though, for some time, you have been aware of its approach, I venture to say that it is far bitterer than you expected. . . . I can assure you that months and months of heartrending anguish are before you. . . . Yet take the bitter cup with both hands,

> and sit down to your repast. You will soon learn a secret, that there is sweetness at the bottom.[26]

Some of the sweetness at the bottom of the cup surfaced years later when Sarah and Adoniram married and continued serving together in Burma.

I found such hope in that tender story. And I love the image of sweetness at the bottom of a bitter cup, waiting for the faithful to discover it.

But I love even more the image of the Savior *filling* a bitter cup with sweetness—transforming the entire cup from one that was bitter into one that testifies of His power and goodness. Creating a cup that overflows—every drop of it sweet.

Some of the cups we are called on to drink in this life are not sweet—are, in very fact, bitter beyond anything we could imagine. The Savior is uniquely qualified to know every drop of the most bitter cup. After all, He held the bitterest cup ever known as He pressed against the soil of Gethsemane in the most important prayer ever offered.

The dregs of that cup were so excruciatingly bitter, according to the Gospel writer Matthew, that Jesus cried, "O my Father, if it be possible, let this cup pass from me" (Matthew 26:39). Mark reported the incident in an even more poignant way, writing that the Savior reasoned, "Father, all things are possible unto thee; take away this cup from me" (Mark 14:36).

But Jesus didn't simply know how bitter the cup was. He also knew the work He had been sent to do—and He knew that finishing that work entailed draining every drop of that bitter cup. So, after the heartfelt plea hoping for release, the Savior told His Father, "Nevertheless not my will, but thine, be done" (Luke 22:42). He drank the bitter cup. He did it for you. For me. For all of us who would ever live.

Jesus described that experience in His own words when He told the Nephites on the American continent, "I have drunk out of that bitter cup which the Father hath given me, and have glorified the

26. kristybruce, "The Bitter Cup," Theology Along the Way, February 20, 2020, https://theologyalongtheway.org/2020/02/20/the-bitter-cup/.

Father in taking upon me the sins of the world" (3 Nephi 11:11). In other words, He also did it for His Father, who wants every one of His children to come back home.

He did it for His Father, who knew that the Savior was the only way for any of us to make our way back to our Father.

It's not difficult to identify the sweetness that replaced that bitter cup. It came three days later in the Garden Tomb. It came in a grove of trees in upstate New York. It comes to everyone who has ever lived on this earth in the miraculous gift of Resurrection. It comes to you and to me and to all of us who exercise the gift of repentance and employ the Savior as a merciful mediator.

It comes every day to you and to me and to all of us who turn to the Savior for strength and succor—trusting in Him precisely because of that bitter cup.

Generations of prophets before that fateful night in Gethsemane knew all about that bitter cup. They, just like God the Father, also knew the Savior would drink it. And they also knew that because of what happened in that garden, as Isaiah promised, the Lord would give us "beauty for ashes, the oil of joy for mourning, the garment of praise for the spirit of heaviness" (Isaiah 61:3).

I love the promise of beauty for ashes. I've sometimes sorrowed in heaps of ashes, wondering if all I held dear was destined to destruction. I've also rejoiced as, much to my astonishment, the Savior has given me beauty for those ashes—taken them all on Himself and stretched out His hand to give me hope in their place.

Whenever I think of bitter cups, I remember one that is perhaps second only to the Savior's own—the cup given to Abraham.

When Abraham married Sarah, they wanted children. But children did not come. For decades, the Lord promised them children. Promised them, in fact, that their posterity would number more than the stars in the heavens.

Still, no children came.

For forty years, Abraham and Sarah clung to that promise.

Then nature took its course, and Sarah's childbearing ability ceased. Such a thing would seem to make a bitter mockery of the Lord's promises—and would seem to cause Abraham and Sarah to reject those promises. I think most of us would lose faith at a time like that. I probably would. Maybe you would too.

But still, the Lord continued to promise that Sarah would bear a son. As improbable as it seemed, there it was again: the continued promise of posterity. Abraham and Sarah must have known what I have come to find out—that the Lord *always* keeps His promises. We don't have to worry about *how* He's going to fulfill those promises, because with Him, all things are possible. Even blessing an elderly, barren woman with a fruitful womb.

Abraham was a hundred years old. Sarah was ninety. And then, in what could only be a profound miracle, Isaac was conceived and born.

It's difficult to comprehend how precious that son must have been to his parents, they who had waited so long for him—desperately pleading, faithfully hanging all their hopes on a promise that seemed impossible to fulfill, wondering how they could possibly have found enough favor with God to see such a miracle.

And then this faithful couple was presented with a cup so bitter, it defies all comprehension. Abraham, accustomed by then to the things of heaven, heard the voice of the Lord calling his name. In complete submission, Abraham responded simply, "Here I am" (Genesis 22:1).

What came next could not have been more bitter. The Lord told Abraham, "Take now thy son, thine only son Isaac, whom thou lovest, and get thee into the land of Moriah; and offer him there for a burnt offering upon one of the mountains which I will tell thee of" (Genesis 22:2).

There was no vague, ambiguous language in the Lord's instruction to Abraham. He said Isaac's very name; He specified the place of sacrifice by name. There was no way Abraham could have mistaken what the Lord was asking of him.

I'm not sure any of us can fully imagine how Abraham must have felt at that moment. Could the Lord have possibly asked anything more heartbreaking of Abraham than to kill the son for whom he had waited in faith a hundred years? Abraham's love for Isaac was so powerful that the Lord specifically mentioned that love. Acknowledged it.

And what about Sarah? The scriptures don't reveal how she reacted or what she felt. But as a mother, I can't even comprehend the abject terror and indescribable sorrow that filled her soul as she faced the loss of her only child—a child who represented a miracle. A child who undoubtedly formed a link between her and her God.

The scriptures are precise in detailing what Abraham did. He did not hesitate to obey. He rose early in the morning, saddled his donkey, and gathered the wood for the burnt offering. He asked two young men to accompany him, and the four of them—Isaac still unaware of the true purpose of the journey—started off. After traveling for three days, Abraham saw in the distance Moriah, the place the Lord had designated for the sacrifice.

With steely determination, Abraham told the two young men to wait there with the ass. Offering only the scantest explanation, Abraham told them that he "and the lad [Isaac] will go yonder and worship, and come again to you" (Genesis 22:5). Asking Isaac to carry the wood for the burnt offering, Abraham carried the knife and the means to start a fire, and they set off.

We're not sure when it started to dawn on Isaac, but as they left and were alone together, he asked his father, "Behold the fire and the wood: but where is the lamb for a burnt offering?" (Genesis 22:7).

Perhaps not yet ready to tell his son what was ahead, Abraham simply responded, "My son, God will provide himself a lamb for a burnt offering" (Genesis 22:8). As far as Abraham knew, Isaac was that lamb; it had to have been a heartrending situation. And with that, we are told, "they went both of them together" (Genesis 22:6).

Keep in mind that Isaac was not a toddler or even a child. Not even a teenager. According to Elder Bruce R. McConkie, Jewish tradition held that Isaac was thirty-seven years old at the time.[27] As they arrived at the place of sacrifice, Abraham built an altar, arranged the wood, "bound Isaac his son, and laid him on the altar upon the wood" (Genesis 22:9). As gut-wrenchingly difficult as it was, Abraham was prepared to sacrifice Isaac to the only one he loved more than he loved Isaac—the Lord.

Abraham now shared his bitter cup with Isaac—Isaac, who could have clearly overpowered his 137-year-old father and escaped the horror that was about to happen. The pain in Abraham's heart undoubtedly surpassed any a knife could have inflicted. And what of Isaac? We

---

27. See *The Mortal Messiah* (Deseret Book, 1981), 1:364.

so often focus on Abraham's unquestioning obedience that we might forget that Isaac exhibited the same obedience. Isaac lay still, submitting himself to the will of the Lord and to the impossible task faced by his father. Both father and son clutched an unbelievably bitter cup.

Abraham had already raised the knife in the air when he heard the voice of the Lord, saying, "Lay not thine hand upon the lad, neither do thou any thing unto him: for now I know that thou fearest God, seeing thou hast not withheld thy son, thine only son from me" (Genesis 22:12). There could never be a shred of doubt by anyone, here or throughout all eternity, of Abraham's love of and loyalty to his God.

At that moment, Abraham saw a ram tangled in a nearby thicket. The two men managed to bind the ram and lay it on the altar Abraham had built just moments earlier with what had to have been one of the heaviest hearts among all men. After sacrificing the ram, Abraham and Isaac descended the mountain.

The beauty for ashes, the sweet that filled the bitter cup, was clearly manifest by the Lord in sparing Isaac's life. Even more than that, though, was the fulfillment of the Lord's promise that Abraham's posterity would number more than the stars in heaven. And the overflowing of the sweetness in that cup came from the fact that Jesus Christ, born in a manger in Bethlehem, came into mortality through Abraham's lineage.

Our cups pale in comparison to those of the Savior and of Abraham. Nonetheless, our cups are very real—and very bitter—to us. The diagnosis of a terminal illness. The earthquake or flood or tornado or wildfire that wipes out a lifetime of effort. Infertility. The imploding of a marriage. A missionary who dies in the field. Debt that threatens to overwhelm. A family member taken without warning. The loss of a job. Betrayal. Pain. Hopelessness and helplessness.

In our darkest moments, we might understandably cry out to our Father as the Savior did, pleading for Him to take the cup from us. Supplicating Him to spare us the anguish.

Sometimes He does exactly that. On those occasions, we are left weak and breathless from an intervening miracle that sets us on our feet again, our faces bathed in the warmth of the Light.

But probably more often, His is a more measured response, designed in accordance with His will for us. Elder Neal A. Maxwell provided a meaningful perspective on that when he said, "While most of our suffering is self-inflicted, some is caused by or permitted by God. This sobering reality calls for deep submissiveness, *especially when God does not remove the cup from us.*"[28]

And sometimes it doesn't seem as though the Lord has removed the cup at all. Sometimes we are left in desperation and sorrow, perhaps thinking that our prayers were not heard or that the Lord doesn't care about us, about our plight. If only we had eyes to see, we would recognize that under the Savior's direction, our bitter cup blessed us beyond our ability to foresee or comprehend.

He who knows the beginning from the end knows exactly what will move us more surely toward an end in His presence. And more often than we would like to acknowledge, that process involves a bitter cup. A cup He won't always remove. But a cup that He will give us strength to drink. A cup He will eventually fill to overflowing with sweet.

When the bitter cup is yours, remember the promise. He will give us beauty for ashes—on His terms, according to His timing, always with our greatest good in mind. He will fill with sweet the bitter cup in the way most measured to bring you to Him.

And that is the sweetest of all.

---

28. Neal A. Maxwell, "Put Off the Natural Man, and Come Off Conqueror," *Ensign*, Nov. 1990, 14.

What Tongue My Gratitude Can Tell, O Gracious God of Israel

In 1963 astronaut Gordon Cooper orbited the Earth in the last and longest Mercury spaceflight. He was the first American to sleep in space during the thirty-four-hour mission and the last American to be launched solo into space. As he gazed at the Lord's creation from a perspective few will ever share, he uttered a simple prayer of thanks: "Father, thank You, especially for letting me fly this flight. Thank You for the privilege of being able to be in this position: to be up in this wondrous place, seeing all these many startling, wonderful things that You have created."[29]

Word of his prayer of thanks circled the globe almost as quickly as his spacecraft had. His was a moving and most appropriate acknowledgment of what he—and all of us—have been given.

29. *Congressional Record*, 88th Congress, 1st Session, 1963, 109, pt. 7:9156.

Another poignant story of thanks was published in a newspaper many years ago.[30] One Friday, the District of Columbia police auctioned off about a hundred unclaimed bicycles. As the bidding opened, an eleven-year-old boy made the first bid at one dollar. However, the bidding went much higher, and the eager eleven-year-old did not get that bike.

Each time another bike came up for auction, the same eleven-year-old boy hopefully started things with his bid of one dollar. Each time, the winning bid far exceeded that amount.

The auctioneer noticed that the boy's hope and enthusiasm seemed to soar whenever a racer-type bicycle came up for auction. Finally, there was just one racer bicycle left. When the bidding went to eight dollars, the auctioneer abruptly halted his chant and cried, "Sold to that boy over there for nine dollars!"

The man, who had been auctioning lost or stolen bikes for forty-three years, took eight dollars from his own pocket and walked over to the eleven-year-old boy, asking for his dollar. The boy dug in his pocket and produced the dollar in quarters, dimes, nickels, and pennies.

When the auctioneer gave the bike to the boy, the boy took only a few steps before carefully parking his new treasure. He then went back, threw his arms around the auctioneer's neck, and cried with gratitude.

None of us—not a poor young boy who gathers all his coins, not a dignified astronaut chosen to orbit the earth, not even someone as prominent as a prophet—is exempt from the admonition to express gratitude. Ammon, the dynamic missionary who saved the king's flocks, gave us a powerful example when he said, "Now my brethren, we see that God is mindful of every people, whatsoever land they may be in; yea, he numbereth his people . . . over all the earth. Now this is my joy, and my great thanksgiving; yea, and I will give thanks unto my God forever" (Alma 26:37).

The expression of gratitude is not a one-way street. When he was working in the Church Office Building, Dee F. Andersen—former

---

30. This story was told by Thomas S. Monson. See "Think to Thank," *Ensign*, Nov. 1998, 17–20.

administrative vice president at Brigham Young University—remembered frequently arriving at the parking lot at the same time as a person he had admired for many years.[31] On those days, the two of them often rode the elevator together. While he desperately wanted to say something to the man who had so inspired him, Dee always found himself so tongue-tied that "I could hardly stammer, 'Good morning,' much less, 'Oh, how I admire you,' or 'Thank you for all you have done and are doing for me.'"

Frustrated at his inability to say something meaningful, Dee Andersen finally wrote a brief note in longhand, expressing his feelings of gratitude. And that's where the power of a two-way response is demonstrated. A few days after he delivered his short note, Dee received the following response:

> Dear Dee,
>
> That was one of the sweetest notes I have ever received, and I appreciate hearing from you. I am indeed grateful to be so close to you, and I hope that we may see each other once in a while. May the Lord bless you and assist you in all your efforts. With kindest wishes.
>
> Faithfully yours,
Spencer W. Kimball

In his epistle to the Thessalonians, the Apostle Paul wrote, "In every thing give thanks: for this is the will of God" (1 Thessalonians 5:18). In his sweet and simple prayer, astronaut Gordon Cooper followed the will of God. So did the hopeful eleven-year-old boy whose pocket held a handful of coins too sparse to fulfill his fondest dream. So did a busy prophet who received a modest, heartfelt note of thanks on his way across the parking lot.

The Savior taught a powerful lesson about gratitude when He healed ten lepers. The healing of the ten lepers is a unique healing

---

31. Dee F. Andersen, "Thanks-Living" (Brigham Young University devotional, Nov. 26, 1985), *BYU 1985–86 Devotional and Fireside Speeches* (Brigham Young University, 1986), 48–49; quoted in Rex E. Lee, "Overcoming Ingratitude" (Brigham Young University devotional, Jan. 11, 1994), speeches.byu.edu.

story because the focus of the story is not on the healing but on the reaction of those who were healed and on what happened afterward.

The story began as Jesus entered a certain village and was met by ten lepers who "stood afar off" (Luke 17:12).

In biblical times, *leprosy* was a sort of catch-all term that included a variety of skin diseases. Some were curable and some were not. Some of them—like leukoderma, psoriasis, and vitiligo—weren't very contagious, but others, such as ringworm, were highly contagious. (Incidentally, leprosy, while not common, still exists today and is known as Hansen's Disease; it is a bacterial infection that can be successfully treated with antibiotics.)

The scripture in Luke's Gospel that tells of the lepers standing "afar off" hints at the situation that existed at that time. Lepers in the Savior's day were required to stand far away from any who were not infected because the disease was considered to be exceptionally contagious and very dangerous; even breathing the same air as a leper was considered hazardous.

People with leprosy were considered to be dead and were cast out of society to colonies in the wilderness, where they lived in tents or caves. They could not live with anyone in a house. They were forbidden to come within six feet of any Israelite—and that distance increased to 150 feet if an east wind was blowing. It's difficult for us in our day to imagine such isolation.

At the time of Jesus, lepers were considered unclean, and anyone who touched a leper was also considered unclean. Lepers had to wear certain clothing, keep their heads bare, cover their upper lips, and wear special bells. If anyone came too close, the leper was to cry, "Unclean! Unclean!" as a warning (see Leviticus 13:45).

Adding to the stigma of the disease itself was the fact that rabbis thought leprosy was a punishment from God for moral transgression. And it wasn't just the rabbis—many people also believed the same thing, judging that a victim of leprosy brought the disease upon themselves for sinful behavior. While their own families and friends banished them and treated them with scorn, Jesus traditionally treated lepers with great compassion, not only touching them but also healing them.

Lepers often maintained a required distance but begged for money, food, or other donations from travelers who came into villages or near the colonies. In the incident described by Luke, however, the ten lepers who stood "afar off" from Jesus seemed to know who He was; they addressed him as "Master" and pleaded with Him to have mercy on them (see Luke 17:13). In other words, they were not begging for food or other material goods; they were asking Him to heal them.

We are told that when Jesus saw the ten lepers, He told them to go show themselves to the priests. "And it came to pass, that, as they went, they were cleansed" (Luke 17:14).

Jesus's instruction to the lepers was completely appropriate. He was the only one who could *heal* them of leprosy, which He obviously did, but a priest was the only one who could *declare them clean* from leprosy, which was required by law.

That is when this miracle took on special significance. All ten lepers had been healed—but one, *and only one*, of them, "when he saw that he was healed, turned back, and with a loud voice glorified God, And fell down on his face at [the Savior's] feet, giving him thanks: and he was a Samaritan" (Luke 17:15–16). The Samaritan leper demonstrated his gratitude by the nature of his actions.

What significance—the only one who returned to thank Jesus was a Samaritan, a member of the racially mixed society that was despised by the Jews. The Samaritans had been traditionally shunned and looked down on by the Jews. In other words, the ultimate outsider was the only one who expressed gratitude and glorified the Savior for His gift of healing.

Accepting the praise and gratitude of the Samaritan who had fallen on his face at Jesus's feet, the Savior then asked, "Were there not ten cleansed? but where are the nine?" (Luke 17:17).

Of the Savior's question, President Thomas S. Monson said, "Through divine intervention, those who were lepers were spared from a cruel, lingering death and given a new lease on life. The gratitude expressed by one merited the Master's blessing, the ingratitude by the nine His disappointment."[32]

---

32. Thomas S. Monson, "Pathways to Perfection," *Ensign*, May 2002, 99–100.

Elder David B. Haight put it another way, one that should penetrate our hearts: "How would you like to be part of the 'nine society'? Wouldn't that be something—to be numbered among those who failed to return and acknowledge the Savior for the blessings He had given them?"[33]

In response to the grateful leper, Jesus said, "Arise, go thy way: thy faith hath made thee whole" (Luke 17:19). The other nine lepers had been healed physically, but through this man's gratitude and acknowledgment of Jesus as the Son of God, he was also healed spiritually.

Am I any better? Do I consistently remember to express gratitude for the Savior's never-ending blessings? Do you? Rex E. Lee, former United States solicitor general and former president of Brigham Young University, said, "You know something? I think that report by Luke, of only one leper out of ten who even bothered to come back and say thank you, may be a fair statistical measure of what we might call the human gratitude index—not only 2,000 years ago, but today as well." In fact, he said, "in today's world, ten percent [who express gratitude] would probably be an overly optimistic estimate."[34]

According to President Ezra Taft Benson, "The Prophet Joseph is reported to have said at one time that one of the greatest sins for which the Latter-day Saints would be guilty would be the sin of ingratitude."[35]

In acknowledging that sorry fact, we need to understand that the Lord has *never* stopped being good. Too many have just stopped being grateful.

In his opening address at the October 1955 general conference, President David O. McKay defined gratitude in this way: "Giving thanks means . . . a fulness of thanks, which is the outward expression of a grateful feeling. *Gratitude is the feeling itself.* That is in the heart.

---

33. David B. Haight, "Were There Not Ten Cleansed?," *Ensign*, Nov. 2002, 25.

34. Quoted in Thomas S. Monson, "The Profound Power of Gratitude," *Ensign*, Sept. 2005.

35. Ezra Taft Benson, *Teachings of Ezra Taft Benson* (Deseret Book, 1988), 363.

Thankfulness is measured by the number of words; gratitude is measured by the nature of our actions."[36]

Thankfulness, said President McKay, is the beginning of gratitude, and gratitude is the completion of thankfulness. "Gratitude," he concluded, "is the heart's recognition of kindness that the lips cannot repay."[37]

When it comes to our relationship with the Savior, *gratitude* is the heart's recognition of what we can never repay—our understanding that we owe Him our very lives.

In his transcendent lyrics, Orson F. Whitney penned, "What tongue my gratitude can tell, O gracious God of Israel." The word *gracious* comes from the Latin word for "good will" and means showing divine grace. A gracious person is one who is compassionate, kind, benevolent, merciful, forgiving, tenderhearted, patient, and charitable. All of those characteristics perfectly describe our Lord and Savior, Jesus Christ.

What, then, is the tongue of gratitude? A *tongue* is an intelligible language—a language that can be understood by interpreting the words that are used. Even though men can understand the *words*, sometimes the Lord is the only one who understands the *meaning* of those words.

Clearly the tongue of gratitude is prayer. Prayer is how we "tell our gratitude" to our gracious Savior.

All four books of scripture are brimming with admonitions to thank the Lord often and with a sincere heart. In the thirtieth Psalm, David pledged, "O Lord my God, I will give thanks unto thee for ever" (Psalms 30:12). In another Psalm, we are told with beautiful simplicity, "Know ye that the Lord he is God . . . be thankful unto him, and bless his name" (Psalms 100:3–4).

In his epistle to the Corinthians, the Apostle Paul proclaimed, "Thanks be unto God for his unspeakable gift" (2 Corinthians 9:15).

The prophet Alma urged, "Counsel with the Lord in all thy doings, and he will direct thee for good; yea, when thou liest down at

---

36. David O. McKay, "An Expression of Gratitude," in *Conference Report*, Oct. 1955, 4; emphasis added.

37. McKay, "An Expression of Gratitude," 4.

night lie down unto the Lord, that he may watch over you in your sleep; and when thou risest in the morning let thy heart be full of thanks unto God; and if ye do these things, ye shall be lifted up at the last day" (Alma 37:37).

And in our dispensation, the Lord told Joseph Smith, "And he who receiveth all things with thankfulness shall be made glorious" (Doctrine and Covenants 78:19).

Do we use the "tongue of gratitude" to express thanks to God "for his unspeakable gift"? Do we speak with words to express feelings only the Lord can understand as we articulate gratitude for the rich blessings so abundantly bestowed upon us? President Russell M. Nelson reminded us that the first thing we should do in the morning is offer a simple prayer of gratitude.[38] Who among us cannot do that?

One of the most pressing reasons for expressing our gratitude is one articulated by Elder Neal A. Maxwell: "God has no distracting hobbies off somewhere in the universe. We are at the very center of His concerns and purposes."[39] His attention is focused on us. We are His work and His glory.

Sadly, we have all heard of people who, when confronted by adversity, have cursed God. You might know some of them. Because it's part of mortality, each of us will come face-to-face with adversity, and when that happens, a life-altering question arises: How will we react?

Scattered across the opening pages of the Book of Mormon, we see examples of some of the ways people react to difficult circumstances. In almost every case, Laman and Lemuel murmured and turned their backs on the Lord. In almost every case, Nephi sought the Lord, exhibiting faith in Him and calling upon Him for help. At one point, as their ship was driven back on the waters, Nephi gives us the pattern for reaction when he explains that, despite being bound and physically harmed by his brothers, "I did look unto my God, and I did praise him all the day long; and I did not murmur against the Lord because of mine afflictions" (1 Nephi 18:16).

---

38. See Russell M. Nelson, "Joy Cometh in the Morning," *Ensign*, Nov. 1986, 67–70.

39. Neal A. Maxwell, "How Choice a Seer!," *Ensign*, Nov. 2003, 100.

The *first thing* the Jaredites did when they set foot on the shores of the promised land was to kneel, humble themselves before the Lord, and "shed tears of joy before the Lord, because of the multitude of his tender mercies over them" (Ether 6:12). It is those tender mercies that are over all those the Lord has chosen—all those He will make "mighty even unto the power of deliverance" (1 Nephi 1:20).

One of my favorite stories of gratitude involves the pioneers of the Martin handcart company. The travails of those courageous pioneers are well known in Church history. Francis Webster, one of the men who survived, crossed the plains with his wife, taking with him no more than he could pile into the handcart he pulled. Addressing a group and displaying great emotion, he said this of his experience:

> I have pulled my handcart when I was so weak and weary from illness and lack of food that I could hardly put one foot ahead of the other. I have looked ahead and seen a patch of sand or a hill slope and I have said, I can go only that far and there I must give up, for I cannot pull the load through it. . . . I have gone on to that sand and when I reached it, the cart began pushing me. I have looked back many times to see who was pushing my cart, but my eyes saw no one. I knew then that the angels of God were there. Was I sorry that I chose to come by handcart? No. Neither then nor any minute of my life since. *The price we paid to become acquainted with God was a privilege to pay, and I am thankful that I was privileged to come in the Martin handcart company.*[40]

In the same meeting, Francis Webster also stated, "Every one of us came through with the absolute knowledge that God lives, for we became acquainted with him in our extremities."[41]

I have faced some extremities; I'm thinking that you have too. Some of my extremities (and probably some of yours too) were blistering. And in those extremities, I came to know the Savior as at no other time in my life. In some of those cases—times when I was at my lowest, when I felt beat up, when I seemed to face certain defeat, when

40. William Palmer, quoted in David O. McKay, "Pioneer Women," *Relief Society Magazine*, Jan. 1948, 8; emphasis added.

41. Palmer, "Pioneer Women."

I doubted my ability to go on—I knew one pivotal fact: Jesus meets us where we are, as we are.

And when He meets us, wherever we are, however we are, we have the opportunity to pour out our heart in the tongue of gratitude. As we do, we find that the trial doesn't become easier—but because He is our Savior, we find that we become stronger.

In those cases, we come to know Him.

And that is one of the paramount reasons for us to be grateful to Him. Forever.

Never Can I Repay Thee, Lord, But I Can Love Thee

Most of us are familiar with the concept of indebtedness. It's really very simple: When we incur a financial debt, we are required to repay the money we borrowed, often with interest. In order to make restitution, or repayment, we need to use currency—in today's world, that's usually in the form of money. The word *repay* can also refer to doing or giving something in return for a kindness or a favor.

That's all pretty straightforward. But the concept of *repaying* the Lord is not such a simple one. As Orson F. Whitney so appropriately noted in his insightful lyrics, we can never repay the Lord. There's such truth in that statement. As King Benjamin told his people, we are indebted to the Lord "forever and ever" (Mosiah 2:24). There are a number of reasons why.

To begin with, the Lord gives us all the blessings of existence—including our agency and our very life. In addressing his people, King Benjamin said of the Savior, "And now, in the first place, he hath created you, and granted unto you your lives, for which ye are indebted unto him" (Mosiah 2:23). Continuing his discourse, King Benjamin pointed out that we were created from the dust of the earth, but even the dust from which we were created belongs to the Lord who created us (see Mosiah 2:25). Then he added a sentiment that might at first seem difficult to believe: "Ye cannot say that ye are even as much as the dust of the earth" (Mosiah 2:25).

King Benjamin wasn't the only one who said so. In the prophet Mormon's great discourse on humility, he said, "O how great is the nothingness of the children of men; yea, even they are less than the dust of the earth" (Helaman 12:7). And in discussing the destruction of Sodom and Gomorrah with the Lord, the prophet Abraham wondered how he even dared to speak to the Lord, as he was "but dust and ashes" (Genesis 18:27).

If that sounds harsh, President Jeffrey R. Holland helped us understand that comparison when he wrote that "hills, mountains, seas, earth" all obey the Savior's voice. "But man does not obey his voice; in willfulness and pride he tramples under foot the words of the Holy One."[42]

The prophet Mormon elaborated on President Holland's point in a discourse that helps us understand the concept with even greater clarity:

> O how great is the nothingness of the children of men; yea, even they are less than the dust of the earth.
>
> For behold, the dust of the earth moveth hither and thither, to the dividing asunder, at the command of our great and everlasting God.
>
> Yea, behold at his voice do the hills and the mountains tremble and quake.
>
> And by the power of his voice they are broken up, and become smooth, yea, even like unto a valley.
>
> Yea, by the power of his voice doth the whole earth shake;
>
> Yea, by the power of his voice, do the foundations rock, even to the very center.
>
> Yea, and if he say unto the earth—Move—it is moved.
>
> Yea, if he say unto the earth—Thou shalt go back, that it lengthen out the day for many hours—it is done;
>
> And thus, according to his word the earth goeth back, and it appeareth unto man that the sun standeth still; yea, and behold, this

42. Jeffrey R. Holland, "Mormon: The Man and the Book, Part 2," *Ensign*, Apr. 1978, 58.

> is so; for surely it is the earth that moveth and not the sun.
>
> And behold, also, if he say unto the waters of the great deep—Be thou dried up—it is done.
>
> Behold, if he say unto this mountain—Be thou raised up, and come over and fall upon that city, that it be buried up—behold it is done. (Helaman 12:7–17)

In other words, the elements—the dust, hills, waters of the deep, mountains, and even the very earth—obey the Lord's voice without hesitation. No questions asked. The Lord speaks, and the elements obey. But we, the children of men, may not be quite as eager to obey. We often hesitate. Question. Weigh what the Lord asks against what we think we know. And in the end, sometimes we obey. Sometimes we don't.

That is why we are less than the dust of the earth.

What about repayment to the Lord? Though we can never get out of the Lord's debt, we should try to repay Him in any feeble way we can. I know I have, and I'm guessing that you have too. But there's a difficult kind of arithmetic at work here: With every effort to repay Him, we are immediately blessed—which then increases our indebtedness to Him even more. Here's how King Benjamin explained it: "He doth require that ye should do as he hath commanded you; for which if ye do, he doth immediately bless you; and therefore he hath paid you. *And ye are still indebted unto him, and are, and will be, forev er and ever*" (Mosiah 2:24; emphasis added).

President Joseph Fielding Smith wrote,

> We will never be able to repay the debt. The gratitude of our hearts should be filled to overflowing in love and obedience for His great and tender mercy. For what He has done, we should never fail Him. He bought us with a price, the price of His great suffering and the spilling of His blood in sacrifice on the cross.[43]

That sacrifice, of course, is part of the enormous debt we owe. The Savior's atoning sacrifice was freely given for all—as another hymn reminds us, "Death is conquered; man is free. Christ has won the

43. Joseph Fielding Smith, *Doctrines of Salvation*, comp. Bruce R. McConkie (Bookcraft, 1954), 1:131.

victory!"[44] All who have ever lived will have body and spirit reunited, "filled with great joy because of the resurrection of the dead, according to the will and power and deliverance of Jesus Christ from the bands of death" (Alma 4:14). And those who properly repent and faithfully endure to the end will have their sins forgiven and will be exalted. Our resulting debt is more than any of us can comprehend.

In his April 2004 general conference address, Elder Joseph B. Wirthlin gave a sweet perspective on the Savior's gift to us:

> How can we ever repay the debt we owe to the Savior? *He paid a debt He did not owe to free us from a debt we can never pay.* Because of Him we will live forever. Because of His infinite Atonement, our sins can be swept away, allowing us to experience the greatest of all the gifts of God: eternal life (see Doctrine and Covenants 14:7). Can such a gift have a price? Can we ever make compensation for such a gift?[45]

President Joseph Fielding Smith emphasized that we can never pay the Savior back. Nor can we ever turn the tables; President Smith emphasized, "We cannot by any number of acts, or a full life of faithful service, place our Savior in our debt."[46]

While it does not pay the incomprehensible debt we owe the Savior, He has given us an indication of what kind of currency we can use as we try to repay Him. The children of Israel were told that what the Lord requires is "to fear the Lord thy God, to walk in all his ways, and to love him, and to serve the Lord thy God with all thy heart and with all thy soul" (Deuteronomy 10:12).

In that declaration, we see four kinds of currency we can use in an attempt to pay our debt to the Lord: fearing Him, obeying Him, loving Him, and serving Him with all our hearts and souls.

We should not mistake *fear* in this context for panic, dread, anxiety, or terror. Instead, to *fear the Lord* is to reverence Him, respect Him, and love Him. Put another way, Elder D. Todd Christofferson

---

44. "He Is Risen!," *Hymns,* no. 199; text by Cecil Frances Alexander, music by Joachim Neander.
45. Joseph B. Wirthlin, "Earthly Debts, Heavenly Debts," *Ensign,* May 2004, 43.
46. Joseph Fielding Smith, *Doctrines of Salvation,* 1:15.

said that fearing the Lord means that we "should so love and reverence Him that we fear doing anything wrong in His sight."[47]

What about giving the Savior gifts as an expression of our recognition of what He has done for us? Anciently, people offered gifts to the Lord when they wanted to worship Him; most often, these were burnt offerings that were placed on the altar of the temple. These offerings were part of the law of Moses and began with Adam and Eve, who were instructed by the Lord to "offer the firstlings of their flocks" (Moses 5:5). An angel later taught them that sacrifices to the Lord were "a similitude of the sacrifice of the Only Begotten of the Father" (Moses 5:7).

Once the Lord made His sacrifice—the Atonement—He no longer required burnt offerings, since the law of Moses had then been fulfilled. Of us, He now wants a different kind of sacrifice: that of "a broken heart and a contrite spirit" (3 Nephi 9:20). That phrase—*a broken heart and a contrite spirit*—appears often throughout the scriptures as well as in counsel and guidance by modern-day prophets and apostles.

As Elder Christofferson taught, "You can offer the Lord the gift of your broken, or repentant, heart and your contrite, or obedient, spirit. In reality, it is the gift of yourself—what you are and what you are becoming."[48]

In a revelation to the Prophet Joseph Smith, the Savior invited each of us individually to come to Him, bringing with us "a broken heart and a contrite spirit" (Doctrine and Covenants 59:8). That measure has great significance: The union of the heart and the spirit constitutes the soul. Giving an offering that involves both the heart and the spirit means that we are giving our "whole souls" as an offering to the Savior, as Amaleki counseled us to do (see Omni 1:26).

Offering the Lord a *broken heart* means that we have shattered—broken to pieces—our stubborn, proud, and willful heart and adopted instead a heart filled with repentance and surrender to His will. As

47. D. Todd Christofferson, "A Sense of the Sacred" (Brigham Young University devotional, Nov. 7, 2004), 8, speeches.byu.edu.

48. D. Todd Christofferson, "When Thou Art Converted," *Ensign*, May 2004, 12.

Neill F. Marriott said, "Paradoxically, in order to have a healed and faithful heart, we must first allow it to break before the Lord."[49]

Significantly, the word *contrite* comes from the Hebrew word meaning "to crush." The *Random House Unabridged Dictionary* describes *contrite* as showing sincere remorse and being filled with the desire for atonement. A *contrite spirit*, then, is more than simply an obedient spirit; it is a penitent soul that regrets past wrongs and feels deep sorrow for any offenses toward God.

President Ezra Taft Benson clarified that concept when he said, "To deny oneself of all ungodliness is to come to Christ by ordinances and covenants to repent of any sins which prevent the Spirit of the Lord from taking precedence in our lives. To deny oneself of all ungodliness is to 'offer a sacrifice unto the Lord thy God . . . , even that of a broken heart and a contrite spirit.'"[50]

Is all of that easy to do? It's easy to *want* a broken heart and a contrite spirit, but it may not be quite so easy to fulfill that desire. The really great things are seldom easy. Most of them require uncommon strength and determination—and, perhaps most difficult of all, a leaving behind of the things that distract us from where we want to be.

In his general conference talk in April 1992, Elder Carlos E. Asay spoke of a "vicious lie" that would have us believe "that it is possible to live successfully and happily . . . with one foot in Babylon and one foot in Zion."[51] And Elder Neal A. Maxwell acknowledged how difficult it can be to bid Babylon farewell—especially when we're tempted to commute there on weekends or even have a summer cottage there.[52]

Sometimes it might almost seem that we are being dragged kicking and screaming to the place we really *want* to be. It's possible to offer a gift with gritted teeth and clenched jaw and to fool ourselves into thinking that it's the *gift* that matters. Not so. The prophet Moroni warned that if we offer a gift grudgingly, it is the same as if we had

49. Neill F. Marriott, "Yielding Our Hearts to God," *Ensign*, Nov. 2015, 32.

50. Ezra Taft Benson, "This Is a Day of Sacrifice," *Ensign*, May 1979, 32.

51. Carlos E. Asay, "Be Men!," *Ensign*, May 1992, 41.

52. See Cory H. Maxwell, ed., *The Neal A. Maxwell Quote Book* (Bookcraft, 1997), 25.

never given it at all (see Moroni 7:5–10). That includes the gift of a broken heart and a contrite spirit.

Giving such a gift against the unfathomable debt we owe the Savior might require some heart surgery—sometimes some extensive heart surgery—but it is completely possible for us to cleanse and purify our hearts and spirits so that we can be moving in the same direction as our Lord and Savior, Jesus Christ. Perhaps before we make such an offering, we might fill our hearts with a love for Him that can't be measured—closer to the love He has for each of us.

His love for you—for all of us—is beyond our comprehension. No matter what is happening in your life, He loves you. No matter how badly broken you feel, He loves you. His astounding love for you drove every act of His life. He threw Himself against the soil of Gethsemane and bled from every pore for you. Your name was on His lips as He hung in agony.

When He died on the cross, He loved you. When He rose again three days later, He loved you. And He is coming back to claim you because He loves you.[53]

For you, for me, for all of us, even though we can never repay Him, we can offer Him our gratitude—express thanks for *His* gift to *us*—by loving Him from the depths of our broken hearts and contrite spirits.

53. From Kathryn Jenkins Gordon, *You Are Loved* (Covenant Communications, 2017), 3.

Let My Lips Proclaim Thy Pure Word

Author, historian, and Unitarian minister Edward Everett Hale, best known for his writings in support of the Union during the Civil War, wrote this about the Savior: "How indifferent are men to this carpenter or that fisherman, who has no word to speak of adventure or of wealth, but has only the word of God to proclaim, and has no credentials but that he comes in the name of the Lord."[54]

To *proclaim* is to announce publicly—usually insistently and proudly—in either speech or writing. It means to praise or extol, to make plain. It means to declare *with great emphasis* something you consider important.

As in all other things of great importance, the Savior provided a perfect example of proclaiming—His sonship, His role, His gospel, His purpose, His loyalty to His Father. Those proclamations are found liberally throughout all four Gospels.

Speaking to the Pharisees in the treasury, Jesus proclaimed, "I am the light of the world: he that followeth me shall not walk in darkness,

---

54. Edward Hale, "How Indifferent," BrainyQuote, https://www.brainyquote.com/quotes/edward_everett_hale_821730.

but shall have the light of life. . . . I know whence I came, and whither I go" (John 8:12, 14).

Many of His proclamations centered on His gospel and His Father. Testifying to the Nephites on the American continent following His Resurrection, He said, "Behold I have given unto you my gospel, and this is the gospel which I have given unto you—that I came into the world to do the will of my Father, because my Father sent me" (3 Nephi 27:13).

The Savior's proclamations were always insistent. Plain. Declared with the powerful emphasis that He knew His message merited. No one who heard Him could go away confused about who He was, what He was here to do, or how He would change the course of history.

There are, of course, many things we could "proclaim." In his inspired lyrics, Orson F. Whitney challenged us to proclaim perhaps the most important thing of all: the Savior's "pure word."

In science, the word *pure* refers to a substance made of just one element that is not mixed with anything else. It is pristine, completely free from contamination. Something that is pure is clear, unclouded, light, and clean. Free from anything that spoils, corrupts, weakens, or pollutes. It is a perfect term to describe all the words uttered by the Savior. Perfect to describe His gospel. Perfect to illustrate all that He proclaimed.

Now it is our turn. We are the ones who are tasked with proclaiming His pure word. But will we do it? Are we able to announce publicly and insistently what we know of the Savior and His word? Prominent Pakistani novelist Umera Ahmed captured the predicament we might find ourselves in: "The most difficult dilemma for a person is perhaps when his heart testifies to an inevitable reality *yet his tongue will not proclaim it*, when his mind screams in acceptance of truth but *he can't bring himself to state it*."[55]

In a day when there is so much pressure from all directions, including all we try to process from social media, do we declare with great emphasis the thing we consider to be of greatest importance? Political economist and journalist Henry George penned advice more

---

55. Umera Ahmed, *Peer-e-Kamil* (Manshurat Publishers and Distributors, 2017); emphasis added.

than a century ago that is even more compelling today: "He who sees the truth, let him proclaim it, without asking who is for it or who is against it."[56]

When we think of those who proclaim the pure word of the Lord, our minds naturally turn to missionaries. The scriptures speak to us of amazing missionaries, some of whom proclaimed the pure words of Christ even before He was born in a manger in Bethlehem—before He worked miracles, before He taught His gospel, before He performed the infinite Atonement. We remember Amulek and the sons of Mosiah. We remember Alma the Younger, who experienced a mighty change of heart when visited by an angel and who spent the rest of his days proclaiming the gospel. We remember Samuel the Lamanite, the fearless prophet who stood atop the city walls and loudly proclaimed his very unpopular prophecy of the Savior's birth, all the while dodging the arrows and stones meant to take his life.

We often hear of remarkable missionary stories in our dispensation, especially in the early days of the Church. Those early missionaries not only demonstrated courage, endurance, and diligence, but they were also great examples of faith and obedience. They left parents, wives, children, grandchildren, and sweethearts to proclaim the pure word of the Lord—often serving long and multiple missions.

My own great-grandfather, who walked alongside a Conestoga wagon to Zion as a teenager, served three missions to his native Sweden after the last of his eight children was born. Each of those missions was bookended by a long voyage across the Atlantic by ship, several of which were rampant with contagious disease. Many died before the ships reached shore. I still have the postcards he sent to my grandmother—his youngest child—that describe the street preaching (and sometimes singing) that he and his companion did. His was bold, persuasive proclaiming. I often wonder whether I would be brave enough to do the same.

Any reflection on early missionaries would be sadly lacking without the story of Elder Parley P. Pratt, who became known as "the Apostle Paul of Mormonism" for his proclamation of Church doctrine.

56. Henry George, "He Who Sees the Truth," BrainyQuote, https://www.brainyquote.com/quotes/henry_george_164054.

If such a thing is possible, he must have had a genetic disposition for proclaiming the pure word of the Lord.

In 1830, before he had ever heard of Joseph Smith or the Book of Mormon, twenty-three-year-old Parley felt a strong prompting to return to his native New York from Ohio to preach the gospel. He and his wife, Thankful, sold their farm at "great sacrifice" and, with only ten dollars between them, boarded a boat in Cleveland, Ohio, that was headed for Buffalo, New York. Parley had faith that if he preached the gospel, the Lord would financially provide for him and Thankful.[57]

At Buffalo, they boarded another vessel headed up the Erie Canal to Albany, New York. Partway through their journey, Parley felt another strong prompting—this time to get off the boat at Newark. He sent Thankful on to their final destination.

Late that summer, Parley was given a copy of the Book of Mormon. Of the book, he wrote, "I read all day; eating was a burden, I had no desire for food; sleep was a burden when the night came, for I preferred reading to sleep. . . . I knew and comprehended that the book was true."[58] Parley contacted Joseph Smith's family and was baptized by Oliver Cowdery in September 1830.

His missionary labors began almost immediately. Within a month of being baptized, Parley was ordained an elder and was called to be a missionary to the Lamanites (see Doctrine and Covenants 32:1–2). Parley and his three companions—Ziba Peterson, Oliver Cowdery, and Peter Whitmer Jr.—left Buffalo and traveled to Kirtland, Ohio, testifying of the Book of Mormon as they traveled. Their message was so well received in Kirtland, he wrote, that "people thronged us night and day, insomuch that we had no time for rest and retirement."[59] More than 120 were baptized. Among them were preacher Sidney Rigdon, who became First Counselor in the First Presidency, and his wife, Phebe.

---

57. *Autobiography of Parley P. Pratt*, Parley P. Pratt Jr., ed. (Deseret Book, 1985), 18.

58. *Autobiography of Parley P. Pratt*, 37.

59. *Autobiography of Parley P. Pratt*, 36.

Following their call from the Prophet Joseph Smith, Parley and his companions then traveled to Independence, Missouri, where they preached to members of three Indian tribes—the Wyandot, Delaware, and Cattaraugus—on what was then the western border of the United States.[60]

In 1835 Parley P. Pratt was called to be one of the original members of the Quorum of the Twelve Apostles in this dispensation. A year later, he and a companion were called to serve a mission in Toronto, Canada. Parley traveled to Canada through Niagara Falls and arrived in Hamilton, Ontario, where he encountered a problem. In order to reach Toronto, he had to cross a large lake—but he was completely out of money and unable to pay for passage on a boat. Walking around the lake would have taken many days and would have been a grueling ordeal. He was in a strange place where he knew no one who might be able to help him, but he was prompted by the Spirit to go to a secret place in the woods and pray for the Lord's help in getting the money he needed to take a boat across the lake.

Concluding his prayer, he walked back to Hamilton and started talking to people there. Within a few minutes, he wrote, "I was accosted by a stranger who inquired my name and where I was going. He also asked me if I did not want some money."[61] When Parley replied that he did, the man gave him ten dollars and a letter of introduction to a religious seeker in Toronto named John Taylor.[62]

Hundreds and finally thousands joined the Church because of that mission. Among those baptized were John Taylor, who became the third President of the Church; his wife, Leonora; and Joseph Fielding along with his sisters, Mary and Mercy. Mary later married

---

60. Richard Dilworth Rust, "A Mission to the Lamanites: D&C 28, 30, 32," in Matthew McBride and James Goldberg, eds., *Revelations in Context: The Stories Behind the Sections of the Doctrine and Covenants* (The Church of Jesus Christ of Latter-day Saints, 2016), 45–49.

61. Parley P. Pratt, *The Autobiography of Parley Parker Pratt: One of the Twelve Apostles of The Church of Jesus Christ of Latter-day Saints* (Law, King, and Law, 1888).

62. See "John Taylor, autobiography, 1858," in Historian's Office, Histories of the Twelve, 1856–1858, 1861, Church History Library.

Hyrum Smith and became the mother and grandmother of future presidents of the Church.

When the Saints were expelled from Missouri in 1838 by the infamous Extermination Order, Parley was arrested when he participated in a battle against Missouri citizens. He spent several months in jail in Richmond and Columbia before escaping and joining the Saints in Illinois. But the break in his missionary service was brief: Just one month after his escape, Parley left on a mission to England, along with most of the Twelve Apostles.

The group started out on August 29, 1839, and traveled more than six hundred miles by carriage before staying in New York for the winter, where Parley had what he called "great success in the ministry." Parley sailed for Liverpool, England, on March 9, 1840, with Brigham Young, Orson Pratt, Heber C. Kimball, and others. After a "rough passage" of twenty-eight days, the group landed in Liverpool on April 6—ten years to the day after the Church was organized.

When he arrived in England, Parley enthusiastically wrote to his wife, "Here is a boundless harvest for the next 15 to 20 years, . . . and here, if the Lord will, I expect to spend 5 or 10 years at least."[63] One can only imagine how such news must have resonated with his wife. As it turned out, Parley served in England for three years, the last eighteen months of which he was President of the Church in the British Isles. During his three-year mission, he was also the editor and publisher of the *Millennial Star.* Thousands were converted to the Church as a result of that mission.

With his characteristic missionary fervor, Parley had a vision of establishing the Church throughout the world. During the early 1850s, he supervised missionary work throughout the Pacific and traveled as a missionary to Chile, where he studied Spanish and became the first missionary in South America.

In the spring of 1844, he was called on a mission to the Eastern states. Shortly after arriving in New York, he was prompted to rapidly return home. When he arrived in Chicago, he learned of the martyrdom of Joseph and Hyrum Smith, and he spent the next few months

---

63. Parley P. Pratt to Mary Ann Frost Pratt, April 6, 1840; Latter-day Saint Church Archives.

consoling the heartbroken Saints until the rest of the Twelve were able to return.

Parley didn't limit his proclaiming the pure word of the Lord to the spoken word. He was a gifted writer who authored books, poetry, newspaper articles, and hymns to teach about and defend the Church. He authored *A Voice of Warning*, one of the most popular missionary books of the nineteenth century, as well as *Key to the Science of Theology*, which explained Church doctrine. His masterful autobiography was published after his death. Among the hymns he wrote are "Jesus, Once of Humble Birth"; "The Morning Breaks"; "Father in Heaven, We Do Believe"; and "Come, O Thou King of Kings."

In 1853, four years before his death, Parley wrote to a childhood friend a letter that demonstrated how the gospel of Jesus Christ had transformed his life; the letter gives us an idea of the sacrifices involved in a lifetime of proclaiming the pure word of the Lord.[64]

"In short," he wrote, "I have been a farmer, a servant, a fisher, a digger, a beggar, a preacher, an author, an editor, a senator, a merchant, an elder, and an Apostle of Jesus Christ." He had crossed the Atlantic six times on missions to England, had explored the western United States, and in Chile had eaten "figs fresh from the trees."

Parley wrote his friend that as a minister of Christ, he had "been honored and received as an Apostle, and scorned as a Devil." Summing up his experiences, Parley wrote, "I have lain months in gloomy dungeons, and been loaded with chains. I have been visited there by visions of Angels and Spirits, and been delivered by miracles."

As I read of his experiences, I know that I too am entitled to visions of angels and spirits as I dedicate myself to proclaiming the pure word of the Lord. You are entitled to the same. As the Prophet Joseph Smith promised, "If you live up to your privileges, the angels cannot be restrained from being your associates."[65] Proclaiming the pure word of the Lord is one of those privileges.

---

64. The following quotes are taken from Parley P. Pratt letter to William Patterson, May 4, 1853, Parley P. Pratt Collection, Church History Library (spelling and punctuation modernized); and Matthew J. Grow, "The Extraordinary Life of Parley P. Pratt," *Ensign*, Apr. 2007.

65. Quoted in Henry B. Eyring, "Sisters in Zion," *Ensign*, Nov. 2020, 67–68.

That proclaiming can happen at any time and in any place. We don't need to receive a mission call or be tasked with serving full-time in order to pronounce with intensity, to declare with great emphasis something we regard as important. And of all those things of which we can testify, the pure word of the Lord is of utmost importance.

Elder Neil L. Anderson expressed it best when he taught the way in which we should proclaim: "If you're not a full-time missionary with a missionary badge pinned on your coat, now is the time to paint one on your heart—painted, as Paul said, 'not with ink, but with the Spirit of the living God.'"[66]

For you and for me, the time is here to both paint and proclaim.

---

66. Neil L. Anderson, "It's a Miracle," *Ensign*, May 2013, 78.

And All My Life Reflect Thy Will

When the Savior concluded His mortal ministry at Golgotha and in the Garden Tomb, He left behind a small but courageous group of Apostles. We who have been taught the gospel and who know of the Savior's life and ministry also know of His Resurrection. We almost take its verity for granted, knowing that all who ever live on the earth will be resurrected, regardless of worthiness. It's one of the gifts of the Savior's Atonement, freely given to every son and daughter of God.

We know that. It's almost second nature to us.

But think for a minute about how the people in Jesus's day felt. Those who served with Him and followed Him had been taught that He would rise again—that His body and spirit would be reunited in the ordinance of resurrection.[67] In teaching His Apostles, He said He would be delivered to the Gentiles, who would scourge Him and put Him to death—but on the third day, He would rise again (see Luke 18:33).

67. For information on resurrection as an ordinance, see *Discourses of Brigham Young*, 397–98, and Spencer W. Kimball, "Our Great Potential," *Ensign*, May 1977, 49.

But the people of His day had never known of anyone who had been resurrected. The entire doctrine must have seemed strange—improbable. Maybe even impossible. In fact, we are told that "they understood none of these things: and this saying was hid from them, neither knew they the things which were spoken" (Luke 18:34).

But it was true, just as was everything else the Savior taught. He *did* rise again on the third day. As the Apostle Paul wrote to the Corinthians, "But now is Christ risen from the dead, and become the firstfruits of them that slept" (1 Corinthians 15:20).

Almost immediately after His Resurrection, He appeared to His Apostles and gave them a sacred commission:

> Go ye therefore, and teach all nations, baptizing them in the name of the Father, and of the Son, and of the Holy Ghost: Teaching them to observe all things whatsoever I have commanded you: and, lo, I am with you alway, even unto the end of the world. Amen. (Matthew 28:19–20)

Those early Apostles who gathered around the feet of the resurrected Christ were not the first missionaries to teach the gospel. Jesus Himself had called two groups of seventy missionaries each and sent them forth, two by two, to go everywhere He would eventually go. They were to teach the people about Him and His gospel. In that role, they acted almost as forerunners, going ahead of the Savior and preparing the people to receive Him.

The Apostles, however—those commissioned by Christ after His Resurrection—were the first to go forth and teach *after* Christ completed His mortal ministry. Among other things, they were to teach of the Savior's Resurrection, bearing witness of an event that must have been difficult for many to accept.

They were commissioned—something more formal and sweeping than a mission call. A *commission* entrusts a person (the Apostles individually) or a group (all of them together) with authority that is granted for a particular function. The Apostles received their commission directly from the Savior, who trusted them with one of the most important matters possible. Having given them their commission, the Savior went to the American continent to visit His "other sheep" there (see John 10:16).

The commissioned Apostles were determined that their lives reflect His will—at all costs. And that cost turned out to be greater than any of them could have realized. All but one died violent deaths for their witness of Christ.

Six of the commissioned Apostles—Peter, Andrew, Philip, James Alpheus, Simon, and Jude—were crucified, just as had happened to their Master on that craggy hill at Golgotha. Crucifixion was universally considered the most horrible form of death.[68] In his pivotal work, *The Life of Christ*, Frederic W. Farrar described the particularly cruel nature of death by crucifixion:

> The feet were but a little raised above the earth. The victim was in full reach of every hand that might choose to strike, in close proximity to every gesture of insult and hatred. He might hang for hours to be abused, outraged, even tortured by the ever-moving multitude. . . .
>
> Death by crucifixion seems to include all that pain and death *can* have of horrible and ghastly—dizziness, cramp, thirst, starvation, sleeplessness, traumatic fever, tetanus, publicity of shame, long continuance of torment, horror of anticipation, mortification of untended wounds—all intensified just up to the point at which they can be endured at all, but all stopping just short of the point which would give to the sufferer the relief of unconsciousness. The unnatural position made every movement painful; the lacerated veins and crushed tendons throbbed with incessant anguish; the wounds, inflamed by exposure, gradually gangrened; the arteries—especially of the head and stomach—became swollen and oppressed with surcharged blood; and while each variety of misery went on gradually increasing, there was added to them the intolerable pang of a burning and raging thirst; and all these physical complications caused an internal excitement and anxiety, which made the prospect of death itself—of death, the awful unknown enemy, at whose approach man usually shudders most—bear the aspect of a delicious and exquisite release. Such was the death to which Christ was doomed.[69]

---

68. See James E. Talmage, *Jesus the Christ* (The Church of Jesus Christ of Latter-day Saints, 1981), 667.

69. Frederick W. Farrar, *The Life of Christ* (A. L. Burt Company, 1874), 640–41.

It's likely that few if any of the Apostles could have known that the Savior would die in such a cruel manner—and it's almost certain that none of them thought such a death would befall them. Jesus Himself prophesied to Peter the manner of Peter's death, but His language was vague (see John 21:18–19), so Peter may not have realized that he too would be crucified. When the time for his crucifixion came, Peter—saying that he was not worthy to die in the same manner as the Savior—asked that he be crucified upside down (in other words, with his head downward).

Andrew was crucified on the northern coast of Greece, which means he had traveled far beyond Judea to preach the gospel after receiving his commission from Christ. (Some wrote that he had preached the gospel as far as modern-day Ukraine.) Like Peter, Andrew considered himself unworthy to be crucified in the same manner as the Savior; he was crucified on an X-shaped cross (now known throughout Christianity as St. Andrew's Cross). He was tied, not nailed, to the cross, and it took him three days to die; he continued to preach the gospel during the three days he hung on the cross.

The crucifixions of the other four of the Savior's Apostles testify to the fact that they too had fulfilled the commission to preach to all the world. Philip was crucified in Hieropolis in modern-day Turkey, where he continued to preach while hanging upside down. James Alpheus was crucified in lower Egypt, after which his body was sawed in pieces. Simon was crucified after ministering with Thaddeus in Persia. And Jude was crucified in Beirut in the Roman province of Syria.

While crucifixion was one of the most barbaric forms of execution, all but one of the other commissioned Apostles also died violent deaths, the locations of which also testify of their determination to reflect the Lord's will to preach the gospel to all the world. Thomas was impaled by a spear near Madras, India. Paul was beheaded in Rome. Matthew was burned to death in Ethiopia. After preaching in Armenia, Bartholomew was skinned alive and beheaded in India. James was beheaded in Rome by King Herod I; he was the first of the Twelve Apostles to be martyred. Thaddeus was shot by arrows in Persia.

The only Apostle who did not die a violent death was John, but he was not spared terrible persecution for his witness of the Savior. While exiled on the Isle of Patmos, he was thrown into a cauldron of boiling oil, which he survived.

Perhaps those Apostles had the strength and determination to follow the Savior's will because of the profound, flawless example He provided of having the faith to put aside His own desires in the bid to do God's will.

Explaining His mission to a crowd of people at Capernaum, the Savior declared, "I came down from heaven, not to do mine own will, but the will of him that sent me" (John 6:38). Following His Resurrection, the Savior told the people on the American continent, "I have suffered the will of the Father in all things from the beginning" (3 Nephi 11:11).

Then came the pinnacle of what Abinadi described as "the will of the Son being swallowed up in the will of the Father" (Mosiah 15:7)—His suffering in the Garden of Gethsemane, His crucifixion on Golgotha, and His burial in the Garden Tomb, from which He rose on the third day. We know that collective suffering as the infinite Atonement.

When Jesus and His disciples reached the Garden of Gethsemane after partaking of the Last Supper, Jesus told the disciples to sit outside the garden and wait for Him while He prayed (see Mark 14:32). He asked Peter, James, and John to go farther into the garden with Him, where He told them, "My soul is exceeding sorrowful unto death: tarry ye here, and watch" (Mark 14:34). He then went about a stone's throw deeper into the garden.

Completely surrendering our will to that of another is not always easy, and it was not easy for the Savior. Trembling at what was ahead, He knew what His sacrifice entailed. It was more terrible than anything any of us can comprehend; it may have even exceeded what He could comprehend. President Lorenzo Snow said that the Atonement "required all the power that [Jesus] had and all the faith that He could summon for Him to accomplish that which the Father required of Him."[70]

His own words provide evidence that Jesus knew how fearful the imminent ordeal would be. Once He was a greater distance into the garden, Jesus fell to His face in incomprehensible agony and prayed, saying, "Father, if thou be willing, remove this cup from me: nevertheless *not my will, but thine, be done*" (Luke 22:42; emphasis added).

Certainly, the Savior would have welcomed another way of accomplishing what He had been sent to do. But setting the perfect example for us, He said, in other words, *Thy will be done.*

And with that, the Father's will was accomplished. We were redeemed, saved from death and hell.

There are others we can look to as examples of those who paid significantly to follow the Lord's will. In 1834, the Prophet Joseph Smith called his father, Joseph Smith Sr., as the Patriarch to the Church. His father pronounced this blessing upon his son's head: "The Lord thy God has called thee by name out of the heavens. Thou hast been called . . . to the great work of the Lord: to do a work in this generation which no other . . . would do as thyself, in all things *according to the will of the Lord*."[71]

Joseph's travails began long before he organized the Church in 1830. Before the age of twelve, his family had experienced the insecurity of frontier farming, poverty, sickness, and death. When he was only seven, Joseph contracted typhoid fever along with his eight brothers and sisters; the disease resulted in a severe bone marrow infection that was healed only through an agonizing surgery that he bore without any anesthesia and that nearly crippled him. He walked with crutches for the next three years.

In July 1830, the Lord told the Prophet, "Be patient in afflictions, *for thou shalt have many*; but endure them, for, lo, I am with thee, even unto the end of thy days" (Doctrine and Covenants 24:8; emphasis added).

---

70. Clyde J. Williams, comp., *The Teachings of Lorenzo Snow* (Bookcraft, 1984), 98.

71. In Gracia N. Jones, *Emma's Glory and Sacrifice: A Testimony* (Homestead Publishers, 1987), 43–44; emphasis added.

The Lord's will has come in such magnificent measure to relatively few in the history of mortality—and few endured more trials and affliction in following that will than did Joseph Smith. He and Emma seldom had a home of their own; they were forced to move from one place to another to escape persecution and so that Joseph could continue the work of translating the Book of Mormon. Six of their children died in infancy. Their family was continually beleaguered by financial struggles.

Joseph was often in jeopardy of losing his life; among other things, he was beaten, tarred and feathered, poisoned, unjustly imprisoned, and once even sentenced to die by firing squad. In early November 1838, the Prophet and six other men were incarcerated in a temporary jail in a log house in Richmond, Missouri, where they were chained ankle to ankle and closely guarded by nearly a dozen guards. On December 1, Joseph and his six associates were moved to Liberty Jail, where they spent the next four months.

In the jail ironically named *Liberty*, the conditions were abominable. The jail's dungeon, where the seven were kept, was bitterly cold and filthy; the men were forced to sleep on bare stone. The ceiling of the dungeon was so low that Joseph—who was a little more than six feet tall—could not stand upright. They were fed rotten, tainted, and sometimes poisoned food. At least once, they were given food that was said to be human flesh, which the jailers called "Mormon beef"; the prisoners refused to eat it.

Comforting the servant who was determined to do His will, the Lord told Joseph, "My son, peace be unto thy soul; thine adversity and thine afflictions shall be but a small moment; and then if thou endure it well, God shall exalt thee on high; thou shalt triumph over all thy foes."[72]

As we know, Joseph Smith spent every day doing the will of the Lord from the age of fourteen until he took his final ragged breath. He paid the ultimate price for his devotion when he was killed by a mob at Carthage Jail on June 27, 1844. He died a martyr's death,

72. *History of the Church,* 3:293; later canonized in Doctrine and Covenants 121:7–8.

sealing his testimony with his blood and paying tribute to his Savior and Redeemer.

There are so many others we can look to for strength in following the Lord's will. We can be assured that there is always a purpose to His will. Think of Lehi and his family—the eight years they spent in the Arabian wilderness might be seen as an almost insurmountable affliction until we consider that it prepared them to establish the New World. And what of Moses and the children of Israel? They suffered for forty years in the wilderness, making them strong enough to inherit and build the promised land.

We are no different. In the Sermon on the Mount, as He taught us how to pray, the Savior addressed His Father in what we have come to know as the Lord's Prayer. He gave us a divine blueprint for our own prayers when He uttered, "Thy will be done in earth, as it is in heaven" (Matthew 6:10).

They are four simple words: *Thy will be done.*

But they may not always be as simple to practice. I've learned that it takes more than just a bucket of faith to turn my life over to the Lord, to forsake my own will, to rely on Him. Especially when I'm in the thick of a desperate situation that is tearing at my very soul. *Especially* when I think I know what's best for me and it's not happening like I think it should.

And therein is the challenge in bending our will to that of the Lord: He will never coerce or force us to do so. It's something we have to do completely on our own. While serving as a missionary, Alma the Younger realized he could not coerce people to repent or change their nature, something that would violate the precious gift of agency. His words on that occasion are sobering and insightful. He declared, "I know that [the Lord] granteth unto men according to *their desire,* whether it be unto death or unto life; yea, I know that he allotteth unto men, yea, decreeth unto them decrees which are unalterable, according to *their wills,* whether they be unto salvation or unto destruction" (Alma 29:4; emphasis added).

Each of us is in charge of our own destiny. We will receive that which we ultimately choose. The famous author and theologian C. S. Lewis profoundly explained, "There are only two kinds of people in the end: those who say to God, 'Thy will be done,' and those to whom

God says, in the end, '*Thy* will be done.' All that are in Hell choose it. . . . No soul that seriously and constantly desires joy will ever miss it."[73]

Along with *Thy will be done*, there is a second simple phrase that acknowledges the Lord's will in our lives: *But if not.*

When Shadrach, Meshach, and Abed-nego refused to bow down and worship a golden image, King Nebuchadnezzar threatened to throw them into a burning, fiery furnace. Still, they refused to worship the idol. He then taunted them by asking, "And who is that God that shall deliver you out of my hands?" (Daniel 3:15).

The three young men, filled with complete confidence in their God, quickly responded that if they were cast into the furnace, "our God whom we serve is able to deliver us from the burning fiery furnace, and *he will deliver us out of thine hand*, O king" (Daniel 3:17).

That demonstrated a real level of faith. But on its heels came an expression of deep, true faith: "*But if not*, . . . we will not serve thy gods, nor worship the golden image which thou hast set up" (Daniel 3:18; emphasis added).

But if not.

What does that mean? It means you trust God to do what's best for you, even if it doesn't turn out like you want it to. It means you admit that you don't understand all things, but He does. It means you know your power is limited, but His isn't. It means you buy in to His plan for you. It means you will reflect His will, even if you aren't able to see ahead enough to calculate the possible consequences.

Here's what else it means. Even if God doesn't do what you know He can do—cure your sickness, repair your relationship, redeem your loved one—you still trust Him.

Even if God doesn't answer your desperate pleas the way you want Him to, you still love Him. You still obey Him. Christian writer Greg Morse posed this question:

> Will we, after praying to him about our deepest pains and sorest bruises, after casting burdens upon him so heavy that they daily threaten to break our will to go on—will we, after experiencing sor-

---

73. C. S. Lewis, *The Business of Heaven: Daily Readings from C. S. Lewis*, Walter Hooper, ed. (1984), 142; see also Doctrine and Covenants 88:32.

> row so paralyzing that we have trouble to even cry—will we, along with . . . three young Jewish boys facing a fiery furnace, defiantly say, "But if not . . ."?[74]

The key is to sincerely ask that His will be done . . . and to know that *if not*—if you don't receive whatever it is you are so desperately wanting right then—you will still inherit all He has for you.

As Satan and his "pinched, calculating little minions" try to oppose your determination and darken your experiences, cling to these words from President Jeffrey R. Holland:

> I believe that in our own individual ways, [the Lord] takes us to the grove or the mountain or the temple and there shows us the wonder of what His plan is for us. We may not see it as fully as Moses or Nephi or the brother of Jared did, but we see as much as we need to see in order to know the Lord's will for us and to know that He loves us beyond mortal comprehension.[75]

What it comes down to is this: the Lord's will is paramount. Sometimes it's easy for us to forget that when we get consumed in our own will. Elder David A. Bednar taught that righteousness and faith are instrumental in moving mountains and in healing the sick, deaf, and lame—but that those eventualities must be in accordance with the Lord's will. Thus, he said, "even if we have strong faith, many mountains will not be moved. And not all of the sick and infirm will be healed. If all opposition were curtailed, if all maladies were removed, then the primary purposes of the Father's plan would be frustrated."[76]

As important as it is that our lives reflect the Lord's will, as Orson F. Whitney wrote in his magnificent hymn, perhaps we can take that to a higher level. President Brigham Young taught, "When the will, passions, and feelings of a person are perfectly submissive to God and His requirements, that person is sanctified. *It is for my will to be*

74. Greg Morse, "But If Not: Walking into Suffering with Faith," Desiring God, June 18, 2018, https://www.desiringgod.org/articles/but-if-not.

75. Jeffrey R. Holland, "Cast Not Away Therefore Your Confidence" (Brigham Young University devotional, Mar. 2, 1999), 6, speeches.byu.edu.

76. David A. Bednar, "Accepting the Lord's Will and Timing," *Ensign*, Aug. 2016, from a Church Educational System devotional, "That We Might 'Not . . . Shrink,'" delivered at the University of Texas at Arlington on March 3, 2013.

swallowed up in the will of God, that will lead me into all good, and crown me ultimately with immortality and eternal lives."[77]

In teaching us what we need to do to be ultimately crowned with immortality and eternal life, Brigham Young went a step beyond submissive—a leap past reflecting, or even obeying, the Lord's will. He created for us a sublime image of where we might most hope to be: *swallowed up in the Lord's will.*

The verbiage he used was not original to Brigham Young. In describing to his people the Atonement of Christ—an event that was still in the future for them—Abinadi said of the Savior, "Yea, even so he shall be led, crucified, and slain, the flesh becoming subject even unto death, the will of the Son being *swallowed up in the will of the Father*" (Mosiah 15:7; emphasis added).

In this, as in all things, the Savior is our Exemplar, showing us by His own life the way to exaltation. At every point in His life, His actions demonstrated that He was totally in—completely consecrated.

How does swallowed up in the Lord's will differ from reflecting the Lord's will or obeying the Lord's will? Elder Neal A. Maxwell taught, "Being 'swallowed up' means being totally enveloped—without question, protest, reservation, or resentment. It is 'all the way,' not halfway. Choosing such spiritual submission is the highest act of deliberate, individual will."[78]

Failing to be *all the way in* reminds me of the image of standing with "one foot in Babylon and one foot in Zion."[79] The danger of that, taught Elder Robert D. Hales, is that "spiritual pedaling takes both feet! Unless you are fully engaged in living the gospel—living it with all of your 'heart, might, mind and strength'—you cannot generate enough spiritual light to push back the darkness." And in today's world, he said, "darkness is never far away. In fact, it is always just around the corner, waiting for an opportunity to come in."[80]

---

77. Brigham Young, in *Journal of Discourses*, 2:123; emphasis added.
78. Bryan Richards, "Mosiah 15:7," Gospel Doctrine, https://www.gospeldoctrine.com/book-mormon/mosiah/mosiah-15.
79. Carlos E. Asay, "Be Men!," *Ensign*, May 1992, 41.
80. Robert D. Hales, "Out of Darkness into His Marvelous Light," *Ensign*, May 2002, 71.

President Holland created an amazing analogy: "The future of this world has long been declared; the final outcome between good and evil is already known. There is absolutely no question as to who wins because the victory has already been posted on the scoreboard. The only really strange thing in all of this is that we are still down here on the field trying to decide which team's jersey we want to wear."[81]

If we're all in, totally swallowed up, we know exactly which jersey to wear.

But what does it all mean? If we allow *our* will to be swallowed up in the will of *the Lord*, do we somehow risk losing our individuality? Won't we in essence surrender our agency by doing what someone else says we should? Elder Neal A. Maxwell eloquently answered that concern when he taught, "Most forms of holding back are rooted in pride or are prompted by the mistaken notion that somehow we are diminished by submission to God. Actually, the greater the submission, the greater the expansion!"[82]

I love the way Elder Maxwell put it all in perspective when he said, "The submission of one's will is really the only uniquely personal thing we have to place on God's altar. The many other things we 'give' are actually the things He has already given or loaned to us."[83]

I pray we are all eager to plant both feet firmly in Zion, to wear the right team's jersey, and to give the Lord that supreme gift, holding nothing back.

---

81. Email correspondence from Jeffrey R. Holland to John Bytheway, June 1, 2004, quoted in John Bytheway, *When Times Are Tough* (Deseret Book, 2004).

82. Neal A. Maxwell, quoted by Henry B. Eyring, in *On Becoming a Disciple Scholar* (Deseret Book, 2009), 61–62.

83. Neal A. Maxwell, "Swallowed Up in the Will of the Father," *Ensign*, Nov. 1995, 24.

Chasten My Soul Till I Shall Be In Perfect Harmony with Thee

Jonah—whose name means "dove"—is the only Old Testament prophet who ministered completely on foreign soil. He was born and raised in a small village about three miles north of Nazareth approximately eight centuries before the Savior was born.

When the Lord became distressed over the wickedness in Nineveh—an ancient Assyrian city in modern-day northern Iraq, more than five hundred miles east of Jonah's home—He called Jonah to go to Nineveh and preach repentance to the people there. But Jonah was afraid. He considered the wicked residents of Nineveh to be his enemies and feared what might happen to him if he went there.

Instead of going to Nineveh, as the Lord had asked, Jonah fled. He went to Joppa, an ancient port city near present-day Tel Aviv, paid the fare, and boarded a ship headed for Tarshish, more than 2,500 miles from Israel *in the opposite direction* from Nineveh. Jonah's intentions were clear: Tarshish was the most remote destination available to him, and there he would hide from the Lord.

Serious trouble arose during the journey when the Lord caused a "mighty tempest" to arise in the sea, so ferocious that it threatened to destroy the ship (see Jonah 1:4). It was perhaps similar to the tempest on the Sea of Galilee that put the Savior and His disciples in danger of extinction or the one that threatened Lehi and his family as they sailed for the promised land.

As would be expected, the mariners aboard the ship on which Jonah sailed panicked and threw everything they could into the sea in an effort to lighten the vessel. Still, the tempest raged. Throughout the storm and during all the frenzied activity on board, Jonah was in the bottom of the ship, sleeping. Finally, the shipmaster woke Jonah and asked him to "call upon thy God, if so be that God will think upon us, that we perish not" (Jonah 1:6).

Believing that someone on board had offended the Lord and stirred His anger, the men decided to cast lots to find out who was bringing such evil upon them. The Jews often cast lots when an important decision needed to be made, much as we flip a coin today; they used objects like coins, stones, and polished sticks as "lots." The Lord Himself often determined where the lots fell (see Proverbs 16:33). That day, the lot "fell upon Jonah" (Jonah 1:7).

Jonah confessed that he had fled from the Lord, and the men asked what they should do to calm the mighty storm and save not only the ship but their very lives. Jonah acknowledged that the tempest was his fault and told those on board to throw him into the sea (see Jonah 1:12). Reluctant to do so, the men rowed as hard as they could to try to bring the ship to shore, but the tempest was too strong. Finally, they cried unto the Lord, begging Him that they would not be found guilty of shedding innocent blood. They then threw Jonah into the sea. The sea immediately "ceased from her raging" (Jonah 1:15).

The rest of the story is one of the most familiar in the Old Testament. The Lord had prepared a "great fish"—probably one similar to a whale—and it swallowed Jonah. Jonah remained in the belly of the fish for three days and three nights, where he cried to the Lord in repentance. Once Jonah vowed to do what the Lord had asked, the Lord "spake unto the fish, and it vomited out Jonah upon the dry land" (Jonah 2:10).

The Lord then asked Jonah a second time to go to Nineveh. It doesn't take much to imagine that Jonah was no longer prone to ignore or flee from the Lord. This time, he went, and the Lord blessed him with not only success but also safety throughout his ministry.

Jonah is famed for more than his experience in the belly of the fish. He was a powerful missionary who turned the entire population of Nineveh—a city of about 120,000 people—back to God. As anyone who has served a mission or preached the gospel in any capacity knows, that would be no small feat. And according to the Gospel writer Matthew, Jonah is the only prophet Jesus likened to Himself: Jonah's experiences with the fish represented the Savior's death, burial, and resurrection.

It's easy to imagine that Jonah would not forget his experience at sea. I certainly wouldn't be able to forget something like that. I don't think you would either. Here's the pivotal question, and it's critical that we understand the answer: Was the Lord *punishing* Jonah for ignoring His request and running away?

No. To punish is to inflict a penalty on someone for an offense. It's to treat someone in an unfairly harsh way. It's to subject someone to severe, debilitating treatment. According to *Webster's Dictionary*, it's to cause someone "pain, loss, confinement, or death as a penalty for some offense or fault." Interestingly, in its comprehensive word project, Princeton University included in its definition of *punishment* to "smear the body with tar and feathers."

One could certainly argue that what happened to Jonah was punishment. It could be considered the penalty (being swallowed by a great fish) for an offense (running away from the Lord). It could definitely be considered severe and debilitating. And it wouldn't be a stretch to say that Jonah was subjected to pain, loss, confinement, and possible death.

Then why wasn't the Lord *punishing* Jonah?

Because the Lord was *chastening* Jonah. And there's a big difference.

That entire difference lies in motive. To *chasten* is to have a restraining or moderating effect on someone; to subdue and humble, not to castigate, beat, or scourge. To chasten is to refine someone, to make one purer in style, not to discipline or penalize. While chastening *can* sometimes be painful, the Lord's purpose in chastening us is to inspire us toward holiness and sanctification—to help us eventually measure up to His image and likeness. It's not to subject us to something so extreme that we'll never repeat *that* mistake again.

The Lord was *chastening* Jonah. The Lord hoped to humble Jonah, to bring him to a recognition of ways in which he could be a more effective prophet, be more fit for the Lord's kingdom. He did not want to terrorize, flog, or destroy Jonah. He wanted, in the most sublime way, to save Jonah.

He wants to chasten all of us in the same way; as Paul told the Hebrews, "Whom the Lord loveth he chasteneth" (Hebrews 12:6). He goes on to say that if we are not chastened, we cannot consider ourselves members of the Lord's family (see Hebrews 12:7–8). And when we *are* chastened, wrote Paul, that chastening "yieldeth the peaceable fruit of righteousness" (Hebrews 12:11).

In his inspired lyrics, Orson F. Whitney pleaded, "Chasten my soul till I shall be in perfect harmony with Thee." *Harmony* is defined as forming a pleasing and consistent whole—as coming to a peaceful agreement. As Paul said when writing to the Corinthians, "He that is joined unto the Lord is one spirit" (1 Corinthians 6:17) with Him. Who among us would not exult in that kind of harmony?

While there are many examples of the Lord's chastening throughout the scriptures and even in more recent times, one of the most powerful is what happened to the Prophet Joseph Smith when he was translating the Book of Mormon. Joseph carried the gold plates to Harmony, Pennsylvania, when he and Emma moved there to be closer to her family. In February 1828, Martin Harris—a wealthy and prominent landowner from Palmyra, New York—arrived in Harmony to be Joseph's scribe as the plates were translated.

The work was intense, requiring hours of focused effort every day on the part of both Joseph and Martin. Martin was donating more than just his time. Harris gave of his considerable wealth to help sustain Joseph and Emma during the translation, and he later mortgaged his substantial farm to pay for the first printing of the Book of Mormon. (Unable to pay the mortgage, he eventually lost his farm.)

By June 1828, 116 pages of the Book of Mormon had been translated. According to the Prophet, the pages were an abridgment of the book of Lehi that had been prepared by Nephi, who wrote that "after

I have abridged the record of my father then will I make an account of mine own life" (1 Nephi 1:17).

By that time, Martin's family—especially his wife, Lucy—had become skeptical. Some of Martin's family were not certain they believed that there were gold plates being translated at all. Lucy herself was unhappy about the amount of time Martin was spending with Joseph on a project she was no longer sure she supported; she was especially upset that Martin was spending the family's money on the project.

Wanting his family to bury their skepticism, Martin repeatedly asked the Prophet if he could take the 116-page manuscript home and show his family what he had been doing. Joseph reminded Martin that he had been instructed by the Lord to show the plates and the manuscript to no one unless the Lord instructed him to do so. Martin relentlessly persisted. Finally, Joseph prayed and asked the Lord for permission—twice. Both times, the Lord told Joseph he was not to let Martin take the manuscript.

When Martin continued to press, Joseph asked the Lord a third time—and this time the Lord gave His permission. Joseph reluctantly loaned the 116 manuscript pages to Martin, extracting from Harris a promise that he would show the pages to no one other than his wife, parents, brother, and sister-in-law. Martin then took the pages to Palmyra with a promise to return with the manuscript on a certain date.

After Martin left, Joseph was preoccupied when Emma gave birth to their first child, who was stillborn. Following the birth, Emma became extremely ill, and Joseph had to nurse her back to health. When he finally had the time and energy to think about the manuscript again, it was past the date by which Martin had promised to return with the manuscript to Harmony.

Joseph traveled to Manchester and asked Martin for the manuscript pages. Martin admitted that he had not only shown the manuscript to people outside his family but that he had lost it. The Prophet, who felt that he shared responsibility for losing the manuscript pages, was horrified. There were a variety of theories as to what happened to the manuscript, including that it was given to friends, it was stolen from the Harris's house, it was disposed of in some other way, or that

Lucy Harris hid it. The most popular theory was that Lucy, annoyed by not being able to see the plates, burned the 116-page translation. To this day, no one knows what really happened.

There was a bit of punishment involved in the incident, though it was not exacted by the Lord. Lucy had kept the manuscript locked in her chest of drawers; Martin, wanting to show the manuscript to a friend, was unable to find the key and picked the lock. The Prophet's mother wrote, "When Mrs. Harris returned, and discovered the marred state of her [chest of drawers], her irascible temper was excited to the utmost pitch, and an intolerable storm ensued, which descended with the greatest violence upon the devoted head of her husband."[84] The Prophet's mother was apparently so horrified that a man would break into his wife's bureau of drawers that she titled the associated chapter "Martin Harris's Perfidy" (*perfidy* meaning treachery, deceit, or betrayal). Somehow it seemed to Lucy that the broken lock was worse than the loss.

Joseph immediately retired to pray for forgiveness—not only for losing the manuscript but for petitioning the Lord repeatedly even though he had already received an answer. He also asked to be forgiven for not heeding the Lord's warning about loaning the manuscript to Martin Harris the first two times he prayed. Joseph then received his chastening: He lost the ability to translate for a season, and the angel Moroni took the plates and the Urim and Thummim away from him for a time.

Martin Harris also received his chastening: A portion of Martin's crops were mysteriously destroyed by a strange, dense fog unprecedented in summer months. The crops on nearby farms were not damaged.

The third person involved in the incident, Martin's wife, was also chastened. Shortly after the manuscript was lost, Lucy Harris separated from her husband.[85] She died just six years later at the age of forty-four.[86]

---

84. Lucy Mack Smith, *History of the Prophet Joseph Smith by His Mother Lucy Mack Smith*, comp. R. Vernon Ingleton, 2nd ed. (Stratford Books, 2006), 122–23.

85. Thomas L. Cook, *Palmyra and Vicinity* (*Palmyra Courier-Journal*, 1930), 206.

86. Rhett Stephens James, "Lucy Harris: Toward a Compassionate Reinterpretation," *Nauvoo Journal* 9, no. 1 (1997): 49–58.

What were the results of the Lord's chastening?

After repentance and renewed humility gained through the chastening, the Prophet Joseph Smith was again given the plates and the Urim and Thummim on September 22, 1828, though he was instructed not to retranslate the lost pages. Since he finished his translation of the Book of Mormon in 1830, more than eighteen million copies have been printed throughout the world in twenty seven languages.

Martin Harris became one of the Three Witnesses of the Book of Mormon and, as such, was given the privilege of seeing the gold plates and the angel. Though he was excommunicated from the Church, he never denied his testimony of the Book of Mormon.

And Lucy Harris, saying she eventually received a vision testifying of the truth of the Book of Mormon, donated $28 to the translation and publication of the plates.

I have occasionally been chastened—sometimes for lesser mistakes, a few times for greater offenses. During those greater times, probably much like Jonah in the stomach of the whale or Joseph without the ability to translate, I felt the deep remorse of having disappointed the Lord. After being chastened, I felt much as Jonah must have felt on his way to Nineveh—much as Joseph must have felt once again taking up the sacred work of translation. Closer to, perhaps even in harmony with, the Lord.

And much like they must have felt, I was humbled in the Lord's unfailing efforts to guide me toward increased holiness. It is that way for all of us if we will but recognize Him in the chastening.

Make Me More Worthy of Thy Love

At first, this line in the hymn made no sense to me—I had always been taught that the Lord loves me with a complete, all-encompassing, never-ending love. A love so fierce that it is beyond my mortal ability to comprehend.

I still believe that.

In fact, at this point in my mortal probation, with a myriad of experiences under my belt, I believe that without reservation. I believe it even on days when I feel distressed. Discouraged. Broken. I believe it even on days when I feel that nothing I do matters. That *I* don't matter. That no matter how hard I try, I still fall short. I believe it even when I feel unloved by everyone else.

I might be incomplete in many ways. Despite that, the Lord loves me completely. I am also imperfect in many ways. Despite that, He loves me perfectly. Even in times when I think I have strayed beyond His all-encompassing love, He loves me still.

And it's not just me. You and I and *all of us* are recipients of that love. He knows you. He knows your name. He knows your heart. He knows your situation. He trod the winepress for you. He threw Himself against the unyielding soil of Gethsemane and bled at every pore for you. Your name was on His lips as he hung in agony. He did it all for you because He loves you. As American author and minister Max Lucado wrote, the Savior is the "maker of the stars" who "would rather die for you than live without you."[87]

As He died on the cross, He loved you. When He rose again as He promised, He loved you. And He is coming back again to claim you because He loves you. *Nothing you ever do or feel can affect that love for you.* His love for us could not be greater, regardless of who we are, what we are, and what we have done. By virtue of that, we are *always* "worthy" of His love.

If you struggle to believe in the Savior's all-encompassing love for you, turn to the scriptures, because they are filled with stories that illustrate the profound love the Savior has for all of us. One of the most touching of those for me is the story of Lazarus, who died and was entombed while his sisters, Mary and Martha, waited for the Savior to arrive.

The experience involving Lazarus consisted of many rich layers. Lazarus fell ill, and his sisters believed that Jesus could heal him. They sent for the Savior with a sense of urgency, explaining how sick Lazarus was and that he desperately needed a blessing; they also expressed their faith that Lazarus could be healed by the Savior.

Mary and Martha waited in vain for the Savior to arrive while they kept a bedside vigil next to their dying brother. Christ had received their message, but He deliberately waited to respond. He intentionally delayed His arrival until He knew Lazarus was dead because He wanted to teach a profound lesson. He wanted to raise the dead, a foreshadowing of what would soon happen when He would rise after three days.

After waiting two days, Jesus set out on foot for the home of Lazarus, Mary, and Martha. As He approached, Mary stayed in the house, but Martha rushed out to greet the Lord, telling Him that *had He come earlier*, Lazarus would not have died (see John 11:21). Jesus subsequently learned that by then Lazarus had been dead for four days, that he had been entombed, and that family and friends had started arriving to comfort the grieving Mary and Martha.

---

87. Max Lucado, *Traveling Light* (Thomas Nelson Inc./Harper Collins, 2009).

As soon as Jesus saw Mary weeping for her brother, the Savior "groaned in the spirit, and was troubled" (John 11:33). He did not groan because He regretted His decision. He did not groan and feel troubled because He somehow miscalculated the timing of His arrival. He groaned and felt troubled because His love for His friends was so deep that He could not help but share in their sorrow—just as He always shares in your sorrow and mine.

When Jesus asked where they had laid Lazarus, Mary and Martha, besieged with grief, led Him along the dusty path leading to a tomb that had been hewn out of rock. What followed is described in the shortest verse in all of scripture—one that is also the most compassionate and loving: "Jesus wept" (John 11:35).

The tears shed by Jesus at the entrance to the tomb demonstrate the Savior's love for each one of us. When we feel any measure of sorrow, He cries *with us*, just as He cried that day with His friends.

You know what happened next; it was one of the Savior's most profound miracles. He commanded Lazarus to come forth, and even though Lazarus "stinketh: for he [had] been dead four days" (John 11:39), he came forth from the tomb, very much alive and still wearing his graveclothes.

As stunning as that miracle was, the great miracle for each of us is the love that our Savior feels for us—every one of us. The crowd of people gathered around the tomb of Lazarus witnessed firsthand something we still know to this day: There is no end to the depth of compassion, empathy, and love poured out for each of us every time we are weighed down by the anguish, adversity, sin, and pains of this life. We are guaranteed that intense love, in fact, in every condition in which we might find ourselves.

Every condition? Yes.

Does that mean He loves us even when we sin? Yes. Even then. As Max Lucado wrote, "He knew the price of those sins was death. He knew the source of those sins was you, and since He couldn't bear the thought of eternity without you, he chose the nails."[88] *That's*

---

88. Max Lucado, "On Easter: The Hands of Jesus, Nails, and the Promise of His Death on the Cross," *Fox News*, Apr. 4, 2021, https://www.foxnews.com/opinion/easter-jesus-nails-death-cross-max-lucado.

how much He loves all of us, even in our sins. Knowing that our sins would cause us spiritual death, He stepped forward and offered Himself as payment so we could live. So we could one day live with Him and our Father.

Sister Linda S. Reeves, former second counselor in the General Relief Society Presidency, reflected on the story of Lazarus when she taught, "Whatever sin or weakness or pain or struggle or trial you are going through, He knows and understands those very moments. He loves you! And He will carry you through those moments, just as He did Mary and Martha."[89]

Along with the Savior's everlasting love for us is the truth that He will never forget us. The Lord Himself promised, "I will not forget thee. . . . Behold, I have graven thee upon the palms of my hands; thy walls are continually before me" (1 Nephi 21:15–16). With the crucifier's nails, each of us was engraved on the Savior's palms by name—each of us earning a place in His heart that could never be erased.

What, then, was lyricist Orson F. Whitney thinking when he penned "Make me more worthy of Thy love"? If we believe all that we read in holy writ and all that has spilled from the mouths of modern-day prophets, the Lord loves us more deeply, more completely, than we can ever comprehend. His is not a merit-based system; He doesn't love us only when we're good or obedient. He loves us *no matter what,* and His love for us will never fade.

We cannot dismiss this line of Orson Whitney's hymn as a slip of the tongue or pen. As an unintentional statement. No, he was far too literate to make such an error. He was a chancellor of the University of Utah, published biographies of Lorenzo Snow and Heber C. Kimball, and penned *The History of Utah.* Additionally, he authored almost ninety poems, personal essays, and lyrics, including the ones we examine here.

He was also remarkably well-educated in the gospel and its doctrine. He filled three missions for the Church, presiding over the European Mission in the last of those. He served as bishop of Salt Lake City's Eighteenth Ward for twenty-eight years. And in 1906, he

---

89. Linda S. Reeves, "The Lord Has Not Forgotten You," *Ensign*, Nov. 2012, 120.

was called to be a member of the Quorum of the Twelve, a position he honorably filled until his death in 1931.

No, this precise wording could not have been a mistake. He meant every word of it.

I wish I could talk to Orson Whitney—sit with him in a quiet, peaceful space, perhaps a cool, shady bowery like the ones where early members of the Church gathered before they had more permanent structures. There I would search his heart, ask him what he meant when he pleaded in his hymn, "Make me more worthy of Thy love."

But that's not possible. Almost a hundred years ago, Orson Whitney cut the tethers binding him to mortality and took his place in the world of spirits, where I have to think he is laboring still for the Savior he so loved.

It is up to me, then—up to all of us—to ponder what was on his mind as he wrote the last lines of his exquisite lyrics.

I've pondered this on many a sleepless night, and what I've arrived at is this: Because the Lord loves us with a ferocious love that can never pale, we must make ourselves worthy of that love *in our own eyes*. We must come to believe that we have value. That we are of eminent worth. That as we struggle through the complicated exertions of mortality, we are deserving of His love. That *we are enough*.

In this sometimes-convoluted stage of our existence, we need to accept that our "worthiness" is not based on what we deserve or have earned, but that we savor and accept the infinite worth of our Savior's love because we are infinitely worthy of it. We need to understand that because the Savior atoned for us, each of us was born worthy of His love—and nothing can change that.

What I'm suggesting—and, if I'm right, what Orson Whitney is suggesting—is that this is easier said than done. After all, he felt strongly enough about it to include it in his hymn. If you're like me, you're subject to all kinds of worldly influences that pretty vigorously convince you that you're *not* worthy of the Savior's love (or sometimes anyone else's, for that matter). But never forget this powerful truth: Your worthiness of the Savior's love can *never* be based on your perceptions. What you perceive and what you feel about yourself can *never* change the fact that the Savior has already reckoned you as worthy.

We have commanding and carefully worded testimony that the Savior never changes. In his epistle to the Hebrews, the Apostle Paul wrote, "Jesus Christ [is] the same yesterday, and to day, and for ever" (Hebrews 13:8). Using almost identical words in his description of the Savior, Nephi recorded, "For he is the same yesterday, today, and forever" (1 Nephi 10:18). The prophet Moroni wrote that "he is unchangeable from all eternity to all eternity" (Moroni 8:18) and that He "is the same yesterday, today, and forever, and in him there is no variableness neither shadow of changing" (Mormon 9:9).

What that means is this: Jesus cannot love you with His all-encompassing love one day and then take that love from you the next day because you make a mistake or even commit a serious sin. It would be impossible. If He did, He would cease to be the Savior. As Alma described the Lord, "I perceive that it has been made known unto you, by the testimony of his word, that he cannot walk in crooked paths; *neither doth he vary from that which he hath said*; neither hath he a shadow of turning from the right to the left, or from that which is right to that which is wrong; therefore, his course is one eternal round" (Alma 7:20; emphasis added).

And finally, we have the most convincing testimony of all. Jesus Himself revealed to the Prophet Joseph Smith that He is the same "yesterday, today, and forever" (Doctrine and Covenants 20:12).

Listen to Him. Don't listen to anyone who says that you are worthy of the Savior's love based only on what you accomplish; if you do, you will believe that you're not worthy unless someone else says you are. Don't listen to those who say you are worthy of His love only if your behavior or character make it so; if you do, you will believe that you're not worthy unless you earn it. Neither of those is true.

You are worthy right now, as you are. And you will be worthy every other day of your life, no matter what. That conviction has the power to change your life.

Think of what that says about you. Christian singer and songwriter Lauren Daigle wrote a song in which she addresses Jesus. The lyrics describe how we might feel as we try to contemplate our worthiness of His love: "You say I am loved when I can't feel a thing. . . . And I believe . . . what You say of me."[90]

That's your job and my job and the job of all of us—to believe what the Savior says about us. I'm betting you believe Him in every other way—that just as your name is engraved on His palms, His words are engraved in your heart. It's our job to take those words and use them to forgive ourselves. To strive to be a little bit better. To endure all we are given with grace and strength. Recognizing that you are worthy of the Savior's love doesn't mean you are perfect; it means you love Him and you acknowledge His endless love for you. And all of us—regardless of the circumstance in which we find ourselves—can do that.

As you strive to recognize your own worthiness, be careful what you listen to—there are voices from every direction that will try to convince you otherwise. Of those, perhaps one of the most thunderous voices is your own. You must especially be aware and careful of the things *you* say about yourself. As author Brené Brown put it, "The most dangerous stories we make up are the narratives that diminish our inherent worthiness. We must reclaim the truth about our lovability, divinity, and creativity."[91] You must change your narrative. When you do, you can recognize how worthy you are of His love.

Author Tony Fahkry put it another way when he said, "I often overhear people declare how they'll feel worthy once they have [a certain thing or person]. You'll never [feel] worthy even with a surplus of money or love if you carry your unworthiness around like a handbag."[92]

If you need to find your worthiness when it comes to the Savior's love, write different narratives. Speak of yourself with great care in the quiet, reflective moments. Reclaim the truth about yourself. Throw out the handbag. Brené Brown gave great advice when she challenged us to "[engage] in our lives from a place of worthiness. It means

90. Lauren Daigle, Paul Mabury, and Jason Ingram, "You Say," *You Say*, 2018.

91. Brené Brown, *Rising Strong* (Random House, 2017), 75–76.

92. Tony Fahkry, "You Are Already Worthy Despite Your Beliefs About Yourself," *Medium*, Jan. 10, 2018, https://medium.com/the-mission/you-are-already-worthy-despite-your-beliefs-about-yourself-488a2a4d5394.

cultivating the courage, compassion, and connection to wake up in the morning and think, *No matter what gets done and how much is left undone, I am enough.*"[93]

When it comes to the Savior's love, I am enough. So are you. I am lovable. So are you. I am worthy. So are you. That will never change.

Nor will His love.

93. Brown, *Rising Strong*, xix.

Conclusion: And Fit Me for the Life Above

More than five decades have passed since I soldiered my way through four years of seminary. At my high school, seminary was practically a given; almost all the students at the high school—two thousand strong—took seminary. Even many who were not members of the Church took it right along with those of us who were.

The seminary building was perched on a beautiful grassy area at the far north end of the high school, only about twenty yards from the door—but, as law required, not on school property.

I loved it.

As my senior year began, I wasn't able to fit seminary into a schedule filled with so many other classes, both required and elective. I'd already completed three years of seminary, I reasoned, which meant I had fulfilled the expected "requirement." But I wanted to finish four years, which left me only one choice: I had to enroll in "early-morning" seminary.

I was acutely aware, even then, that many youth living outside Utah had only one option for seminary: 6 a.m. in the nearest meetinghouse, which was often what seemed a shocking distance for those of us in Utah Valley. After all, we were accustomed to a church on practically every corner. Students and teachers alike in those out-of-state areas usually had to be on the road by 5:30 a.m.—sometimes even a little earlier. But the early hour made it possible for students to be back at the high school in time for the day's classes to start.

Though I had been a member of the Church all my life, my gospel experience was still somewhat immature. I *heard* about those beyond-the-pale seminary classes out "in the mission field" and shook my head at how hard it must have been to make that kind of commitment. But I realize now that I had little real comprehension of the principle of sacrifice.

The sacrifice required to attend our early-morning seminary seemed wimpy in comparison. Seminary started at 7:30 a.m.; because the seminary building was right next door to the high school, we didn't have to start any earlier than that. Seminary classes were dismissed at 8:20, giving us plenty of time to get to our homerooms by 8:30 when school started.

Those years in seminary were precious to me. We went through the standard curriculum: Book of Mormon, Old Testament, New Testament, and Church history. In the ninth grade, I had an exceptional teacher who made the characters in the ancient Americas come alive. In addition to the scriptures, I learned some profound nuggets here and there that are still with me all these years later.

One of them was about the Final Judgment, an event that seemed impossibly far away yet struck fear and trepidation in our adolescent hearts. One wintry day—as the sun was still hanging on to the horizon, not quite ready to make the leap into the sky over the rugged mountains framed by our classroom window—our seminary teacher said, "You know, I think we might partially judge ourselves to determine which kingdom we'll inhabit."

A collective gasp of disbelief—or was it simply surprise?—washed over the room.

Judge ourselves?

The teacher had been sitting on the corner of his desk, chatting somewhat amiably, as he normally did. As the repercussion of his statement rumbled through the room, he suddenly stood. I think he could tell right away that none of us had been prepared for what was to us a revolutionary concept.

He went on to explain, and what he said became one of those nuggets that I still ponder. His reasoning went something like this: There are those who are totally comfortable being in a smoke-filled bar, swilling a beer, exchanging crude remarks, punctuating their conversation with one profanity after another, surrounded by others who did the same. We weren't to determine whether that was good or bad, appropriate or inappropriate. We were simply to envision that person.

Now, he said, do you think that person would be comfortable in sacrament meeting, dressed in suitable Sunday attire, partaking of the emblems of the sacrament, and hearing music and spoken words testifying of the Savior? Or what about this: Would that person be comfortable in the temple?

Or how about this: Do you think the person who feels peace and tranquility in sacrament meeting or the temple would be comfortable in a bar?

The light started to dawn. Perhaps, he was suggesting, each of us will inherit a degree of glory that will reflect not only what we earned but what we most desire. We will *want* to be in a place where we feel comfortable after our time in mortality ends, just as we want to be comfortable now.

Then our teacher took his metaphor to the next level. He asked, "Do you think a person who lived a celestial life would be comfortable in the telestial kingdom? In the same way, do you think a person who lived a telestial life would be comfortable in the celestial kingdom?"

I'm guessing that at our relatively young age, the students who sat around me and who made the effort to come to school an hour early for seminary were all trying—or at least wanting—to live a celestial life. Most of us wanted to serve missions, marry in the temple, serve in the Church, and do the other things that earmarked us as righteous members of the Church. Some of us already had experience with feeling the Spirit, and I'm pretty certain that all of us wanted that to be a regular occurrence in our lives.

I'm also guessing that none of the students around me wanted to hang out with the crowd in the bar. (At least, I couldn't fathom that anyone was likely to *admit* that, even if they entertained the thought.)

We got it. We understood what the teacher was trying to convey. We grasped the concept that how we behaved not only ticked every item on the checklist of salvation, but it also made of us people who would eventually seek out a place—an environment—that would be comfortable for us. And that place would not be the same for everyone.

None of us will be alone at that Final Judgment. The Lord will be there with us. The scriptures are clear in telling us that He is our judge. In his epistle to the Hebrews, Paul wrote, "The Lord shall judge his people" (Hebrews 10:30). The Lord Himself said that "mine arm shall judge the people" (2 Nephi 8:5). We are told that Jesus Christ is a righteous judge (see Moses 6:57) and that He will judge all things (see Doctrine and Covenants 77:12).

We also know that as part of that process, the Lord will advocate for us with the Father (see 1 John 2:1). The Lord Himself said, "I am your advocate with the Father" (Doctrine and Covenants 110:4). In fact, only six months after the Church was organized, Jesus Christ revealed through the Prophet Joseph Smith that "I am in your midst, and am your advocate with the Father" (Doctrine and Covenants 29:5).

As our Judge and Advocate, the Lord will look at the whole of our lives, take into consideration all factors and extenuating circumstances, and from that determine which glory, or kingdom, we will inherit. But going back to the concept my seminary teacher shared, it seems likely we will also be involved—beyond answering for our behavior on earth, that is. For in addition to giving an accounting—accepting liability for the bad and recognizing the good—our hearts will yearn for what we desire. For that place where we will be most comfortable, where we most *want* to be.

I imagine that you and I are very similar. That you and I yearn with all our hearts to be where the Savior and His Father are. To be with our families in a place of everlasting joy.

If that's the case, we need to start preparing *now* to live as they live. To be with them. To do those things that make of us men and women who are acceptable to Them—who can live in harmony with the way They live. To be completely comfortable in Their presence. In other words, as Orson Whitney wrote, to be "fit . . . for the life above."

There's more to the equation than simply *where we want to be.* After the Lord told the Prophet Joseph that He was our Advocate with the Father, he specified that "it is [the Father's] good will to give you the kingdom" (Doctrine and Covenants 29:5).

Let that profound truth settle in your heart. We must never forget that Heavenly Father's plan is to return us home to Him. It has always been that way. That's what He wants more than anything for you, for me, and for all of His children. President Henry B. Eyring taught, "But he loves you, wants you to be with him, and knows you must have a mighty change in your heart, through faith on the Lord Jesus Christ, humble repentance, and the making and keeping of sacred covenants."[94]

But we must also never forget that Satan's plan is to keep us from ever going home again. This is no simple game. He wants to destroy us—*all* of us. To keep us far from our Father.

So how can we, in our mortal sphere, start now to become fit for the life above—the one we want with all our hearts? The life that keeps us pointed toward the Father and His glory? The one that fits us as one who will live in harmony with the eternal family God is building?

I'd like to suggest just a few things we might consider as we ponder how we can become fit for the life above. As you ponder and pray, you will undoubtedly come up with other ideas specifically tailored to your circumstances.

Perhaps it would be wise to begin with the concept of being *fit*. In his lyrics, Orson Whitney pleads with the Savior to "fit me for the life above." The word *fit* means "proper and appropriate"—the way in which we strive to guide our thoughts and behaviors. The word *fit* also means "adapted to" or "suited." If we are to inhabit the place where our Father is, we must be suited to it—adapted to that divine kingdom in every way.

There's another aspect to fitness as well—being *fit* means having the health, vigor, strength, and adequacy to function at our optimum level. Just as we exercise and build up our physical muscle to become physically fit, so should we exercise and build up our spiritual muscle so we become spiritually fit, to fit us for the life above. Successful physical conditioning requires consistent, regular, planned activities

---

94. Henry B. Eyring, "To Draw Closer to God," *Ensign*, May 1991, 67.

that work all the different muscles in the body. Successful spiritual conditioning requires the same thing: consistent, regular, planned activities that bring us, line upon line, to a spiritual condition in which we can be in the presence of Deity forever.

Spiritual fitness includes being spiritually born of God. Addressing the people of Zarahemla, the prophet Alma posed a series of questions to Church members—fifty-nine questions that are still relevant for us in our day (see Alma 5:6–59). In fact, Alma's questions provide an excellent self-interview that can help you determine where you are in the process of experiencing a mighty change of heart, which is the foundation of spiritual fitness.

Of all the questions Alma asks, perhaps the most profound are these: "And now behold, I ask of you, my brethren of the church, have ye spiritually been born of God? Have ye received his image in your countenances? Have ye experienced this mighty change in your hearts?" (Alma 5:14).

Change is essential to the process of becoming fit for the life above. Writing to the Romans, the Apostle Paul said, "Like as Christ was raised up from the dead by the glory of the Father, even so *we also should walk in newness of life*" (Romans 6:4; emphasis added). Newness of life is characterized by a mighty change of heart that allows you to be a partaker of the Savior's divine nature—to take upon you His characteristics, to become fit for the most exalted life above. The Lord Himself has asked us to make for ourselves a new heart and a new spirit (see Ezekiel 18:31), prerequisites for entering His presence and inheriting celestial glory.

C. S. Lewis provided a glimpse of what that change and newness of heart looks like, explaining that instead of happening instantaneously, it's a process:

> Christ, here and now, in that very room where you are saying your prayers, is doing things to you. It is not a question of a good man who died two thousand years ago. It is a living Man, still as much a man as you, and still as much God as He was when He created the world, really coming and interfering with your very self; killing the old natural self in you and replacing it with the kind of self He has. At first, only for moments. Then for longer periods. Finally, if all goes well, turning you permanently into a different sort of thing;

> into . . . a being which, in its own small way, has the same kind of life as God; which shares His power, joy, knowledge and eternity.[95]

Does it require consistency, great effort, and determination to become spiritually fit? Yes. In fact, there may be times along the way that you pale at the effort required, wondering whether it is worth the investment for something you can envision only by relying on faith. But know this: The effort you expend pays dividends here as well as in the life above. Brigham Young said that "when a person is filled with the peace and power of God, all is right with him."[96]

There's more. Manifestations of spiritual fitness include the fruits of love, joy, and peace (see Galatians 5:22); a heart filled with the Holy Ghost (see 3 Nephi 12:6), who will be your constant companion (see Doctrine and Covenants 121:46); a body filled with light (see Doctrine and Covenants 88:67); and no more disposition to do evil but to do good (see Mosiah 5:12). As you become spiritually fit, the Lord has promised to renew your mind (see Romans 12:2) and give you a heart that will know Him (see Jeremiah 24:7).

Another practice that can help fit you for the life above is a serious study of the scriptures. The word *scripture* literally means "a writing," and was originally used by the writers of the New Testament to refer to the books of the Old Testament (see Matthew 22:29; John 5:39). Today, we use the word *scripture* to describe texts that are recognized by the Church as being inspired and sacred. According to latter-day revelation, *scripture* is used to distinguish those things that are written or spoken under the influence of the Holy Ghost, which then become "the will of the Lord, . . . the mind of the Lord, . . . the word of the Lord, . . . the voice of the Lord, and the power of God unto salvation" (Doctrine and Covenants 68:4).

As you study the Lord's word, you will get to know Him and will eventually be able to be like Him. The Prophet Joseph Smith taught, "If you wish to go where God is, you must be like God, or possess

---

95. C. S. Lewis, *Mere Christianity* (HarperCollins, 1952), 149.

96. Brigham Young, remarks in the Bowery, Great Salt Lake City, July 5, 1857; see *Journal of Discourses*, 5:1–2, and *Discourses of Brigham Young*, 33.

the principles which God possesses."[97] Tad Callister emphasized the importance of studying the scriptures when he wrote, "We become like those things we habitually love and admire. And thus, as we study Christ's life and live his teachings, we become more like him."[98]

In your effort to become one who can live in harmony with God's family, you will find that you strive to become like the Savior—your judge, your advocate, your Redeemer. And as you strive to become like Him, you become fit for the life above. Brad Wilcox, former second counselor in the Young Men General Presidency, said, "Christ asks us to show faith in Him, repent, make and keep covenants, receive the Holy Ghost, and endure to the end. By complying, we are not paying the demands of justice—not even the smallest part. Instead, we are showing appreciation for what Jesus Christ did by using it to live a life like His."[99]

As you have read this book, you might have felt a bit overwhelmed by the progress you still need to make. I know I've felt that way often. Much of what I still need to do motivates me to keep trying—but in my limited, temporal existence, I also find it's easy to get discouraged. At times like those, I like to remember the words of Orson F. Whitney. I hope that his words of solace and encouragement lift you as much as they have lifted me:

> No pain that we suffer, no trial that we experience is wasted. It ministers to our education, to the development of such qualities as patience, faith, fortitude and humility. All that we suffer and all that we endure, especially when we endure it patiently, builds up our characters, purifies our hearts, expands our souls, and makes us more tender and charitable, more worthy to be called the children of God . . . and it is through sorrow and suffering, toil and tribulation, that we gain the education that we come here to acquire and which will make us more like our Father and Mother in Heaven.[100]

---

97. Joseph Smith, *Teachings of the Prophet Joseph Smith,* comp. Joseph Fielding Smith (Deseret Book, 1938), 216.
98. Tad R. Callister, *The Infinite Atonement* (Deseret Book, 2000).
99. Brad Wilcox, "His Grace Is Sufficient" (Brigham Young University devotional, July 12, 2011), 2, speeches.byu.edu.
100. Orson F. Whitney, quoted in Spencer W. Kimball, *Faith Precedes the Miracle* (Deseret Book, 1972), 98.

All of it makes us more fit for the life above—that life where we want to be, where we *can* be because of our Savior, the Redeemer of our souls.

About the Author

Kathryn Jenkins has more than fifty years of professional experience in corporate and internal communications, public relations, media relations, marketing communications, and publications management. She was the managing editor of Covenant Communications, Inc., and has held communications management positions at a variety of national and international corporations. Among other positions, she was the press secretary for Congressman Howard C. Nielson (R-UT); director of public relations at Westminster College in Salt Lake City; director of employee communications at Novell, Inc.; an editor at Brigham Young University Press; vice-president of Aspen West Publishing Company; and an editor at the *Ensign* magazine (now the *Liahona*).

Kathryn is the author of a number of published books for the Latter-day Saint market, including the bestsellers *Scripture Study Made Simple: The Book of Mormon* and *Butch Cassidy and Other Mormon Outlaws of the Old West.* She has also coauthored a number of books in the health sciences and emergency medical services field and has written chapters in five compilations. She writes fiction under the pen name of Cassandra Grey.

She wrote an award-winning book-length poetry manuscript that was recognized by the governor of Utah. A former member of Sigma Delta Chi, she was named an Outstanding Young Woman of America. She served on the board of directors of the Utah County Republican Party and the Utah County Mental Health Association and is a member of the Daughters of the Utah Pioneers.

Kathryn's interests include reading, writing, traveling, and doing family history. She has met five presidents of the United States, sailed up the Nile River, prayed in the Garden of Gethsemane, eaten tempura in Tokyo, and received a dozen long-stemmed red roses from a stranger on the street in Athens.

Scan to visit

https://www.kathryn-jenkins.com/